KEYS TO PARENTING THE GIFTED CHILD

Sylvia B. Rimm, Ph.D.

Clinical Professor of Psychiatry
Case Western Reserve University
School of Medicine
MetroHealth Medical Center
Cleveland, Ohio

D0064189

BARRON'S

Cover photo by Scott Barrow, Inc., Cold Spring, NY

DEDICATION

To our children—as they lovingly parent their own children.

© Copyright 1994 by Barron's Educational Series, Inc.

All rights reserved.
No part of this book may be reproduced in any form, by photostat, microfilm, xerography, or any other means, or incorporated into any information retrieval system, electronic or mechanical, without the written permission of the copyright owner.

All inquiries should be addressed to:
Barron's Educational Series, Inc.
250 Wireless Boulevard
Hauppauge, New York 11788

Library of Congress Catalog Card No. 94-6105

International Standard Book No. 0-8120-1820-6

Library of Congress Cataloging-in-Publication Data
Rimm, Sylvia B.
    Keys to parenting the gifted child / Sylvia B. Rimm.
        p.   cm. — (Barron's parenting keys)
    Includes bibliographical references (p.   ) and index.
    ISBN 0-8120-1820-6
        1. Gifted children—United States. 2. Parents of gifted children—United States. 3. Gifted children—Education—United States. 4. Parenting—United States. I. Title. II. Series.

HQ773.5.R55   1994
649'.155—dc20   94-6105
                                                                    CIP

PRINTED IN THE UNITED STATES OF AMERICA
    67   8800   98765

CONTENTS

INTRODUCTION

Parenting our own four gifted children was our introduction to the unique joys and pressures of children who were in many ways both similar to and different from other children in their schools and neighborhoods. There were no books or courses to guide us along the way. Schools were doing little to understand or provide for our children's special learning needs, and parent advocacy had not yet begun in any organized fashion in the communities where we lived. Although gifted educational programs were available in some large cities and university centers, parents of gifted children in small cities, suburbs, or rural areas felt quite isolated when they recognized their children were learning at a different pace and depth than many of their peers.

As parents, we had feelings that were a mixture of awe, doubt, shame, and excitement. The awe and doubt were related to a fear that we as parents could not rely on memories of our parents for strategies because we might not be intelligent enough to understand our gifted children's needs. Sometimes we felt that our children were, indeed, much smarter than we were. We were humbled by their high IQ scores, as are many parents of gifted children. The feelings of shame stemmed from the fear that perhaps we had done something wrong by teaching our children before they were ready to learn. This accusation was frequently directed at parents. Our excitement came from observation of our children's enthusiasm, curiosity, and intensity. They absolutely loved to learn.

Our children are grown now. Our parenting experiences led us to parenting advocacy and guided my own higher education toward the psychology of giftedness. In my Family Achievement Clinics, located in Wisconsin and Ohio, I have worked with many hundreds of gifted children, adolescents, and young adults. I have also worked with their parents and their teachers. This extensive experience has inspired me to share my opportunities with the many parents of gifted children through my books.

We hope that this book of keys helps you to feel less lonely as you parent your own gifted children. It should also help you to feel more confident. You don't ever have to worry about parenting perfectly. This, like other perfectionisms, is not only impossible but is not even normal or healthy. Your gifted children are likely to become learners, thinkers, workers, and contributors to our society if you love them, inspire them toward the joys of learning and thinking, and avoid some of the pitfalls that may mire other parents.

Our own children were taught that their giftedness carries with it a responsibility to make their own small contributions enthusiastically. Regardless of children's talents and intelligences, this is the most important message I believe we need to give all children. In this way, each generation can move our world toward a more positive future.

I thank my children for being our first experiments and my husband for being such an effective partner in our parenting experience. Certainly, I acknowledge all the families and educators with whom I've worked in my clinics, as well as all the parents who have called in or sent their parenting questions to me. Thank you also to my editor, Linda Turner, my reviewers, and, most important, my editorial assistant, Joanne Riedl, for assisting me in communicating clearly and concisely these guidelines for parenting gifted children.

1

SO YOUR CHILD IS GIFTED!

The first moment of holding your infant in your arms is engraved in your memory permanently. Just thinking about that wonderful moment brings a smile to your lips and joy to your heart. Your feeling of joy, however, was unrelated to your child's intelligence, creativity, or talent. It was related only to the wonderful bonding that comes with the miraculous experience of birth.

The wonderment of the initial bonding was mixed with some self-doubt, although by now the doubt may have temporarily disappeared. As mother or father, you may have felt concern about how capable you were of parenting this miraculous child and worry about whether you were truly ready for this new challenge. There were questions, perhaps openly discussed, perhaps quietly felt but unspoken, about how your partner would experience parenting this infant with you. If you were a single parent, you felt the awesome responsibility of being the sole caretaker for your new baby. You definitely were not thinking of your child's talent. Your first wishes were for good health and normalcy.

The first days and weeks of your child's life were filled with the basic activities of feeding, soothing, singing to, observing, and hugging this small bundle. As family and friends gathered around and commented on the baby's resemblances to you, your grandfather, or your mother-in-law, the observations about alertness or the kidding about musical or artistic talent began. These were not intended as communications about giftedness but as humorous comments only. Mainly, your wonderful baby was totally accepted. That was as it should have been and how it should always be.

The developmental needs and tasks of your children should always be at the forefront of your parenting. Your preschool gifted child, your school-age talented child, or your extremely intelligent teenager is always a baby, child, or adolescent first. Giftedness is only a secondary description. When this order is reversed, children suffer from pressures to be what they can't be—intellectual objects of their parents' creation instead of unique human beings.

I believe you know all of this already. You love your children so deeply, and you would not want to use them as merely extensions of yourself. Nor would you want them to develop their capability to think without developing their ability to feel or love. Why, then, must you be reminded of what you already know? It is only because giftedness can be so reinforcing that it can lead even the most conscientious parent astray. Gifted children who learn quickly can become powerfully demanding, and the loving parents who see these children's hunger for stimulation can become enslaved in providing it. Here are some unusual examples:

> Robbie, a high-energy baby, was rocked to sleep by the rhythms of mathematical facts. What began as a humorous game became an exciting challenge and a powerful manipulation. Robbie's hunger for mathematical learning hooked Mother into hours of repeated multiplication and division facts at bedtime. Crying was soothed by math, and although it is true that Robbie exhibited extreme mathematical talent by school age, he was also a peculiarly single-minded and powerful child. Although the rocking mathematics finally stopped, the search for

appropriate mathematical stimulation for Robbie became a burning oppositional issue between parents and school. His unique math talent stole from him an emotionally healthy childhood.

While still in her baby seat, Tanya peered at books as her daddy read to her. Her attention to color and words seemed unusual. Her love for being read to increased and expanded with a thirst that seemed to have no quenching. Mother and Father felt obligated to read to Tanya continuously. Her love of books was varied and extensive, far beyond a typical three year old's. Although wanting to enhance Tanya's interest, both parents became enslaved by a toddler whose hunger for books closed off other facets of her development. Tanya's parents actually believed they had no choice but to continue reading to Tanya as long as she demanded it.

Although rare, these two stories are real. The sometimes pressured but exciting environment that surrounds an extraordinary child who is very stimulated by learning can mislead even a loving, intelligent parent.

Gifted children exhibit talent early. They may speak in whole sentences when other children of similar age know only a few words. Some observe environmental details that aren't even noticed by others. Their questions may reveal a depth of understanding atypical of preschoolers. They may construct complex puzzles or toys or take toys apart in a manner that indicates extraordinary spatial understanding. Unusual sensitivity may be displayed. They may learn letters, numbers, colors, and shapes with speed and interest, come to adultlike mathematical conclusions, read spontaneously, or show extraordinary musical talent far beyond that of typical children. All these characteristics indicate giftedness.

Enjoy and encourage your children's love of learning, but foster their play, responsibility, imagination, affection, and fun so they can grow as whole as well as gifted children.

2

FIRST AND ONLY CHILDREN

Some special parenting issues affect first and only children, especially gifted children, and can enhance their giftedness; others can cause serious problems. Some of these issues make parenting easier, but others make it harder. First and only children are all unique, though, so the descriptors do not fit all of them.

First children are only children for at least a little time until other children are born. Sometimes they are only children for many years. Therefore, they are at risk of being attention addicted and too powerful. With a two-to-one adult-to-child ratio, they easily become the center of adult attention. If you add several grandparents or aunts and uncles, the attention ratio may be multiplied. It's easy to take one child along to adult social functions at which the child may be the center of an adult audience or included in adult conversations. Parents may treat them as consultants: for example, "Where would you like to eat?" or "What would you like to do tonight?" They easily feel equally powerful to their parents and, sometimes, even more powerful. Democracy may begin too early for first and only children. They can't imagine why they require adult guidance when they already feel like one of the adults, and they may not do well sharing attention when other bright children in the family attract the attention of their parents. If they've been only children for a long time, siblings may feel very threatening to them.

Here are some of the more favorable characteristics. First and only children may become very independent. They are frequently good at individual and leadership activities. Because these children are not surrounded by siblings, they may take the initiative to keep themselves busy, interested, and interesting. Unaccustomed to the company of other children, they may not feel as pressured to be part of peer groups and are often willing to take the risk of not conforming to teenage crowds.

You may also wonder what research reports about first and only children. Among the eminent in almost every field, a disproportionately large number are first or only children. Also, in studies of IQ and birth order, on the average oldest children tend to have higher IQs than their younger siblings. To compound the issue further, among underachieving gifted children, more than the expected proportion are only children. There can be only mixed predictions about achievement based on a child being a singlet. Most studies show that oldest children tend not to be underachievers.

Here are some suggestions that can maximize the advantages and minimize the problems of first and only children:

- Be sure to keep an adult life separate from your child's activities. If your child resents not being included, remind your child how fortunate she is to have parents who love each other so much that they continue to enjoy each other's adult company.
- Don't include your child in adult social functions to which no other children were invited.
- Be sure that neither parent includes the child in negative intimate conversation about the other parent, giving your child more adult or more powerful status than a parent.
- Don't feel guilty when you see your child playing alone. This cultivates independence and imagination. Choose a

regular time each day for your child to develop the habit of being alone. Explain to the child positively that he can choose special quiet activities. Also, explain that you plan to use this time for your own personal interests and activities. Show your child how a mechanical timer works, and explain that the buzzer will signal the end of quiet time. The first quiet times should be short; 10 or 15 minutes may be sufficient. Gradually expand the time to at least half an hour. Your child may actually learn to enjoy playing alone and wish to continue even after the timer buzzes. Soon you'll be able to eliminate the timer. Your child may complain of boredom initially but will initiate activities eventually if you ignore the complaints. With time and opportunity, the activities become rewarding in themselves.

- If your child has cousins who are close in age, invite them to spend vacation time with your family.
- If there are no children of similar age in the neighborhood, some taxiing to friends' homes may be required so that your child has practice in sharing adult attention and playing with peers.
- Summer day camps or enrichment programs that require shared attention are especially healthy for preschoolers who are only children.
- Family camps or conservation and learning projects in which your family participates with other families with more than one child can help your child to keep her special status in perspective and also expose her to variations in family structure, for example those with many children or with single parents.
- Try to avoid overprotecting or doing too much for your child. Although it is difficult to know whether you are doing so, you can compare your involvement to that in families you respect who have two or more children.

- Avoid overpraising your child (see Key 27). Too high praise can internalize impossible expectations for your only or oldest child.
- When there is only one child, you may be able to afford more material possessions. Nevertheless, pretend to yourself that you can't, so your child doesn't take for granted the gifts you've already so generously given.
- Don't feel guilty if you have only one child. This child can be a special joy to you just as you are to your child.

3

PARENTING WITH A UNITED FRONT

The term "united front" means that despite differences in preferred parenting styles, adult caretakers should compromise about each other's position so that the view from the children's perspective is of similar expectations, effort, and limits. Gifted children are more likely to be achievers if their parents join together in a united front.

Gifted children are vulnerable to being included in cross-generational alliances with a parent, grandparent, or other adult against the other parent. Parents of the 1990s, who have been encouraged to be open and honest in their communication with their children, may actually be more open, even intimate, with their children than appropriate. They may share with their children or adolescents more adult communication than they can understand. The main problem with such intimate and equal sharing is that it confers adult status to the child too soon. Furthermore, verbally gifted children sound so like adults that they are often perceived as understanding more about life than they actually do.

There is a subtle parent rivalry, hardly ever spelled out in psychology books, that causes problems for families. For the purpose of example, let's examine the traditional two-parent family. Both parents are concerned about being good parents, and because our society is so competitive, this wish to be a good parent is accidentally operationalized as being the "best" parent. If being the best parent doesn't set up contradictions between parents, then it is likely that they'll be able to cope with the competition they feel and come to agreement on values for their children. In an effort to prove oneself best, however, sometimes one parent may cause the other parent to feel that he or she can never be good enough.

One parent may see him- or herself as best by being kind, caring, loving, and understanding; the other parent may see him- or herself as best based on being respected and expecting a child to take responsibility and show self-discipline. Although each parent sees him- or herself in these different ways, the parents do not see each other in the same way they describe themselves. The parent who sees him- or herself as kind and caring is perceived by the other as overprotective. The parent who views him- or herself as disciplined and responsible is seen by the other as rigid and too strict. They unconsciously decide that their own way is best, and they therefore must balance out the other parent by becoming more extreme. Thus, the kind, caring parent becomes more protective to shelter the child from the parent who expects too much. The expecting parent becomes more demanding and expects to balance the overprotective parent. The more one expects, the more the other protects, and the more the second protects, the more the first expects. Oddly enough, parents become more extreme in their positions in the belief that they are doing what is best for their children. The outcome for the children is that one parent actually is too strict and the other is overprotective.

If children are faced with parents who have contradictory expectations and if these children lack the confidence to meet the expectations of a parent, they go for protection to the parent who supports "the easy way out." Kind and caring parents, unintentionally, without recognizing the problem they're causing their children, find themselves continually protecting them. When children have grown up in an environment in which one adult allies with them against another adult to find an easy way out, they develop the habit of avoiding challenge. They fear taking intellectual and psychological risks because there is no united support for risk taking.

To add to the complications in two-parent families, children in our society frequently have more than one caretaker. Sometimes they are reared in families with one, three, or four parents. Grandparents, aunts, and uncles can take on the parenting role. Caretakers may extend to individual child care providers and day care teachers. It's very important to the parenting of children that the adults who guide their lives lead them in a reasonably consistent, united way.

The balancing act increases in complexity with three or four parents. Each is desperately anxious to keep their children's love and may thus not provide the best parenting. They attempt to compensate for the other parent in the direction of either expectation or protection. After a divorce, parents are more vulnerable to parent rivalry. They often believe that they can tempt children to loving them by protecting them most, doing too much for them, or buying them more.

It is not unusual for children also to form alliances with grandparents or aunts and uncles against their parents. Grandparents may act on their own rivalry with their children, and aunts and uncles may sabotage their siblings, sometimes unintentionally and other times to act out their own sibling rivalry. A rather sad joke states that the reason that grandparents get along with their grandchildren is that they have a common enemy—the parents.

Considering the many caretakers in children's lives, it's not possible to have completely consistent expectations, but certainly among the most critical adults, there should be reasonable similarity. If adults are consistent, children know what's expected of them. They also understand that an adult will not assist them to avoid what feels a little hard, scary, or challenging.

Adult-child alliances lead to rituals described as "ogre and dummy" games. One adult unintentionally sabotages and depowers a parent, always causing serious harm to children. When adults respect each other's differences and are willing to make compromises in parenting their children, children can be raised in a healthy, positive environment instead of one that leads them to manipulative power and opposition. Rimm's law summarizes this critical issue:

> As parents, if you can stay united and respect each other and your children's teachers and caretakers, your children are more likely to grow up respecting those who have the important responsibility of leading them.

4

PARENT SUPPORT GROUPS AND NATIONAL ORGANIZATIONS

Because gifted children are a minority, appropriate education is unlikely to be provided unless there is vocal and visible community support. Therefore, parent advocacy is important to your gifted child's education. Gina Riggs, Executive Director of the New Jersey Gifted Child Society, points out that "Parents want for their gifted children the same as all parents want for their children: opportunities to learn all that they are able to learn—no more, but certainly no less."

Whether or not gifted programs are available in your school, you'll want to join or form a parent support group. If there are no such programs, be prepared to be positive, patient, and persevering: a challenge is ahead. Indeed, even if programs are available, these qualities are useful as you try to maintain the good components of present programs and add or change others.

Ideally, in your support for gifted education, you want to model for your children your love of learning and the value you place on education. If schools do not provide quality education, however, there is a risk that your enthusiasm for what you know is important can take you beyond advocate to adversary. Thus, you may find yourself becoming discouraged and even very angry at the schools. Your challenge is to continue to advocate without being so adversarial that you cause more harm than good.

Although you may want to mobilize community efforts on the behalf of gifted children, you may accidentally model oppositional behaviors that can interfere with your children's motivation. If your children perceive a negative or hostile attitude toward schools, teachers, or school administrators, they may easily internalize this as an excuse for avoiding responsibility in academic areas they perceive as boring or irrelevant. They may believe that you condone their avoidance of work because you agree with their perspective on the inappropriateness of assignments or curriculum. Sometimes gifted children become openly hostile or passively aggressive in the belief or hope that their parents will side with them against the teacher or school. Furthermore, they may generalize this defiant behavior to other teachers or future school years when they conclude a curriculum is inappropriate or undesirable.

Parent groups can provide many kinds of support to gifted education. Members can be helpful to each other by sharing personal experiences and providing encouragement during those times of isolation parents of gifted children often experience. Furthermore, they can volunteer to help within school programs and can pool their talents to provide unique learning experiences for their own as well as other gifted children. Support groups can also initiate enrichment programs outside school hours. Some parent groups sponsor Super-Saturdays or evening enrichment classes. Fund-raising for student or teacher activities is always helpful.

Local parent support groups can join state and national organizations dedicated to educating and encouraging gifted children. Members can actively lobby and support legislation for educational opportunities. They can serve on boards of education or local school advisory committees. Conferences and meetings provide further opportunities for parents to learn about giftedness. Most major organizations sponsor annual or biannual conferences, and many state associations sponsor yearly conferences. All associations welcome parents.

New Jersey's Gifted Child Society sponsors a live response hotline called PING (Parent information for gifted) designed specifically for parents of gifted children. It is staffed weekdays between 9 A.M. and 4 P.M. (Eastern Standard Time). The number for parent help is 1 (900) 773-PING. There is a charge for use of the line, although the Gifted Child Society is a nonprofit organization and regards the line as a service to parents rather than a fund-raising effort.

If you don't have a local group, state and national organizations can advise you on how to form one and how to affiliate with an association. National organizations usually provide magazines, journals, bibliographies, and other information on services to help you with your gifted child. (Names and addresses of major associations are listed at the end of the book.)

Your gifted children will gain much if you support their needs through positive advocacy. Your efforts can also benefit other gifted children.

5

~~~~~~

SIBLING RELATIONSHIPS

Sibling relationships cause concern in all families. Even if there's only one child in your family, this key may apply to you. Cousins who are close in age to your only child may provide both companionship and competition similar to that among siblings. You'll also want to be aware that having gifted children in the family may complicate sibling matters.

Some typical sibling relationships that cause special problems for gifted children and suggestions for dealing with those problems are described here.

Gifted Children with Less Talented Siblings

Gifted children with very high intelligence or extraordinary talents may present impossible competition in their areas of giftedness for other children in their families. These children's unique abilities often require inordinate investments of time and resources to develop their talents and meet their unconventional needs. In the process, gifted children naturally receive large amounts of attention and recognition. Brothers and sisters must be able to admire their gifted siblings' successes but also must recognize that similar levels of success may not be attainable for them. Less talented siblings must use a different measuring stick to evaluate their own abilities, or they may fall into the trap of viewing their own real successes (and themselves) as failures. In the words of one successful sibling of a gifted girl,

Once I realized that there was nothing I could do to achieve as well as my sister, I decided to stop competing with her, to do the best I could, and to recognize that what I was doing was really good, too.

Although this youngster came to understand that he could be successful despite his being a "second-place" student, his realization was not automatic. In addition to rewarding the victories of their most gifted children, parents must also recognize the successes of the other siblings in the family, basing this recognition on each child's individual abilities and effort. As difficult as this may sometimes feel, being honest with children about intellectual differences and limitations is better than pretending that children are all the same. You can also encourage your children by reminding them that their employers of the future will not be requesting their IQ scores but will instead be observing their attitudes, initiative, perseverance, and creative thinking. Furthermore, no matter how intelligent people are, they always find others who are more intelligent.

Gifted Children in Families of Other Achieving Gifted Children

It's not unusual to find that all of the children in a family are gifted. This can be genetic or because of a favorable environment, positive parent and teacher expectations, or, most likely, all of these factors. Each child in the family may feel increased pressure to fulfill the expectations set by preceding siblings. The first day of school for the second, third, or fourth child may inevitably begin with, "Oh yes, I know your sister. She was such a good student!" This identification may be pleasing if your children believe they can fulfill the teacher's expectations. The early recognition may even produce privileges and trust that otherwise would take longer to earn. On the other hand, less confident children may perceive this early identification by teachers as a threat. They may worry that their performance will be less impressive than that of their older siblings. Sensitive teachers quickly learn to recognize differences between siblings. You may want to explain to your child that "Although Mrs. Jones had Bryan in her class, she'll soon realize that you're also a good worker but that you're a different person from your brother."

Perhaps most important, parents of several gifted children may need to make a specific effort to ease grade pressures for the younger children. Let them know that you understand the special tensions they may feel as a result of the inevitable comparisons with their siblings. Your message can be that all children in the family are expected to do the very best they can and that their performance will be individually evaluated, not compared with that of their siblings.

Gifted Children with Older Siblings of Lesser Abilities Who Are Close in Age

One of the most difficult relationships between siblings is one in which a younger gifted child has a sibling of average (or lower) ability who is older by only one or two years. As parents you may feel an altruistic commitment to "root for the underdog." Although culturally this attitude is very typical, it can place unpleasant pressure on all your children. It can cause parents to refrain from providing appropriate enrichment opportunities for their gifted children out of fear of embarrassing the possibly insecure older children. For gifted children, this strategy produces both frustration, from the reduced opportunities for skill development, and pressure to underachieve and hide their high abilities. The older children feel the sibling pressure anyway. Often they are also less motivated to achieve because of continual assurance that they are not really expected to achieve at higher levels.

17

A better approach is to reinforce gifted children's achievements, even if this means acceleration to the same grade as the older children. (It's best if the siblings are not in the same classroom.) Also, it's critical that parents reinforce older children's achievements according to their efforts and abilities. As children become mature enough to discuss their differing abilities and the sense of competition they feel, such open discussions help them to deal with their sense of personal worth despite obvious differences in talents, school grades, and academic recognition.

One critical underlying principle should always guide you in decision making: Each child should be provided with the best possible opportunities for intellectual and creative development. A belief in equal treatment in the name of democracy can easily misguide you to withdraw opportunities for gifted children because other siblings are unable to participate. On the other hand, *fair* treatment provides all children in the family with affordable and attractive opportunities that fit their special interests and capabilities. Treating siblings the same can actually exacerbate the competition they feel.

Children shouldn't feel pressured to be the *best* in the family in any arena. The world requires many highly capable people, so there are opportunities for all children. Furthermore, although intelligence certainly matters, what children do with their intelligence is much more important. Feelings of competition within the family should be discussed and accepted but funneled to games and other appropriate, less ego-involved outlets. All members of the family require support from each other in a highly competitive world.

6

SIBLING RIVALRY

One problem that seems almost inevitable and probably exasperates parents most often is the squabbling that takes place among children in the family. Sometimes it even seems that the children can be truly mean to each other. It is frustrating that children whom you love so much can't "just get along together." It feels even more frustrating when they are highly intelligent and should surely know better. Parents find themselves providing endless lectures to their children on how and why they should get along, usually to little avail.

Parents will never be able to make sibling rivalry disappear. Sibling rivalry is a natural response for children who are reasonably assertive. The only time sibling rivalry disappears is when one child gives the orders and the other accepts them. Then, of course, the children don't fight. However, if they're assertive, or if one child expects to give all the orders, most children have differences some of the time. Extreme sibling rivalry is a little more uncomfortable than what typically occurs in families, but you, as parents, can take action to minimize the day-to-day rivalry.

First, insist on time alone for all your children so that they're not always together. If they're always together, obviously they're going to argue more. Separate time alone is also healthy for children's independence, imagination, and confidence.

When your children argue, let them know that you plan to stay out of their arguments unless they hit each other or are too noisy; then you'll become involved. Explain that you won't mediate or try to determine who is right or wrong. You'll never be able to do this anyway. If your children are hitting each other, then ask them to go into two separate rooms for 10 minutes. If they're merely arguing too loudly, ask them to argue in another room so you won't hear the noise.

Eight-year-old Jean Ann described her new relationship with her big brother this way: "We used to nag at each other all the time, but then Mom separated us every time we'd fight, so we just don't do it as much. It's not fun being separated so much." Most siblings truly enjoy being together, although this may not be obvious from the perspective of their exhausted parents.

Remember: If you mediate, you'll only make the problem worse. Each child will try to get you on his or her side, and the fighting will increase. The child you rescue most may be the one who starts the battles. Here are some other suggestions to help alleviate sibling rivalry:

- A reward system can be used temporarily to reinforce children's cooperative behavior. This works particularly well when siblings are required to spend a great amount of time together, for example during summer vacation or a long car ride. By dividing the day into two or three sections, such as early morning to noon, afternoon to dinner or evening meal, and evening meal to bedtime, children can receive a point for each time period of cooperative behavior. Siblings receive a point only if both (or all) children are being nice to each other. This point system encourages their cooperation. The goal is to accumulate a small number of points (10 to 15) toward an activity, such as going out for pizza, going to a movie, or renting a special video. You'll know that your system has been effective when one child hits or teases another and the other says she doesn't mind because it was all in fun. This is real confirmation of your children's cooperation. No system works forever, but this is effective during particularly stressful times. You and your children can also create your own schemes.

- Surprise plans can be used to build cooperation between siblings. When one parent gathers the children together to plan a surprise for the other parent or for another child, then the children become involved in planning toward a goal and feel closer. Alliances with positive goals build children's unity. The secrets of gift giving, surprises, and parties can help unite brothers and sisters and diminish arguing. Special projects or plans for Grandma, Grandpa, Aunt, Uncle, a neighbor, or friend encourage a sense of togetherness that comes from joint efforts. Parents can effectively use cooperative strategies often to build sibling solidarity.

- Sibling rivalry frequently affects children's achievement. Children tend to assume easily that their accomplishments appear more impressive if their brothers' and sisters' performance is not as good as their own. This may mean that your gifted achieving child may be busy graciously (or not so graciously) degrading other children in the family to feel more gifted. Explain to your children that it's nice to have a "whole smart family," and remind them that achievement by one child doesn't limit achievement by the others.

- Most children have feelings of jealousy and should be encouraged to admit them. Teach children to handle these feelings better by accepting the challenge of openly admiring their sisters and/or brothers. This seems to help everyone and can minimize the put-downs. If your children put each other down, don't take sides at the time. However, you should communicate privately your concern to the child who is doing the putting down. Tell the child you'll be noticing his efforts and will give a secret signal when you notice that he is being nice. There's a much better chance of improved behavior if you don't correct the child in front of siblings. Secret signals are powerful.

• Although you want to encourage your children's differing strengths and abilities, don't make the mistake of considering one child the scholar; the next, the jock; the third, the social one; and so on. Although your intention is to give each child a special place, children hear this as a very competitive message. They feel that they must be the best in the family at something. All your children can and should be the best students they can be. In addition, some children may enjoy arts or athletics more than others, and all children should enjoy friendships, although some may be more social than others. The subtle labeling of children based on their particular strengths may only increase the sibling rivalry and make all but the scholar feel that they can't be good students.

• Don't appoint an achiever to the role of tutor for an underachiever. This serves only as a daily put-down for the child being tutored. The tutored child may neither understand nor be able to express her feelings of resentment toward the helpful sibling. Children often say they appreciate their siblings' help, but they also say it makes them feel "dumb."

Be sure to give each child some separate time with each parent, for sports, chores around the house, or cultural adventures. Although activities including the entire family can be the norm, children who lack confidence should not always need to function in the shadow of more confident siblings. Separate father and son activities are particularly important for all sons in the family, although these activities are sometimes difficult for fathers. Most dads probably enjoy having the more positive and confident son around all the time. Nevertheless, if fathers hope to develop positive attitudes in all their sons, each son needs to be with Dad some of the time without the other, or one son may always feel second best. Mothers are often the protectors of their less confident sons, so they should avoid the all too common mistake of feeling sorry for their less confident boys. Don't be surprised to find that a growing confidence in one son may cause another to lose confidence temporarily. Parents may feel as if they are precariously balancing on a seesaw.

What probably helps parents the most is knowing that if they refuse to take sides in their children's arguments, the children eventually become closer. By young adulthood, they will have learned that it's possible to share their parents' love, and finally, they'll truly appreciate their siblings.

7

^^^

GRANDPARENTS

C lose relationships between gifted children and their grandparents are important and often inspirational to the children. As parents, you can help your children value and appreciate their grandparents.

When you talk about your parents (your children's grandparents), emphasize their good qualities and refer to them with respect. Disrespect for your own parents gives your children permission to be disrespectful to both you and their grandparents. You will soon regret your negative communications.

Encourage your children to have one at a time, special visits and trips with their grandparents. This permits both your children and their grandparents to enjoy opportunities to know each other without the grandparental responsibility for significant discipline. You may also want to give the children special permission for treats when they are with their grandparents. If you let your children know that there can be flexibility and exceptions when they visit their grandparents, the grandparents, who might provide the treat anyway, won't be in the position of sabotaging your power. Grandparents may need some written instructions for the general routines to which your young children are accustomed.

If you have some childhood resentment and anger toward your parents, don't share these with your children. Your feelings are most likely too complex for even gifted children to understand, and your children are likely to resent you or their grandparents and feel caught in the middle. Finally, if your parents are ill or aging uncomfortably, encourage your children to help them and to understand the difficult aging process.

Although children's relationships with their grandparents are usually very special, they can also be quite destructive. Here are some do's and don'ts you may wish to share with your parents to guide them in grandparenting your children, whom they undoubtedly love:

- **Do** *love your grandchildren as much as you'd like.* You can't love them too much. If you don't express your love, this is a sad loss for you and them.
- **Do** *stay in close touch.* Telephone your grandchildren directly, or when you're calling their parents, be sure to talk also with the grandchildren. Write letters and send pictures, and encourage the children to do the same. Save the children's letters for them. They will appreciate them when they are grown. If your grandchildren live nearby, arrange regular visits for doing something special. Introduce them to cultural opportunities for which their parents may not have time, or just spend time with them.
- **Do** *give special enriched learning gifts.* Now may be a time in your life when you are able to purchase a set of encyclopedias for your grandchildren that would be too expensive for the parents of young children to afford. Your grandchildren will remember that you're the one who gave them the special gift, and their parents will appreciate your help. If the children's parents can't manage the cost of a computer or a special camp experience, you may also be able to help with those opportunities. If your own finances are limited, sharing some interesting books or toys from your own childhood may provide an in-depth level of enrichment.

- *Do share stories about your own childhood.* Encourage your grandchildren to tape-record your stories. They will have them forever and will always be able to hear your voice. They will appreciate the past and have a better sense of history. Encourage their questions and observations.
- *Do play competitive games with your grandchildren.* Gifted children may be very competitive, so be sure not to let them always win. They should learn to cope with both winning and losing. Children often recall playing cards with Grandma or playing checkers or chess with Grandpa. Games are also a nice way for informal communication just to "happen."
- *Do projects with your grandchildren.* For example, if you play music, knit, crochet, quilt, sew, work wood, or paint, share these interests with your grandchildren. Sharing skills can have a great impact. It makes the children feel closer to you, and they learn to appreciate your talents. Furthermore, they will always remember that a particular skill was taught to them by their grandparents.
- *Do read to your grandchildren.* Encouraging gifted children to love books is always valuable for them. You may wish to share books from your own childhood or from their parents' childhoods. Listen to your grandchildren read to you but only if they enjoy reading aloud. Forcing them to read aloud may cause them to feel pressured.
- *Do listen to your grandchildren.* Let them talk to you and tell you stories. Be an attentive audience. Gifted children often love to talk, and other children may not be as interested or may not be at their intellectual level.
- *Do say positive things about your grandchildren's parents.* If the children believe that you respect Mom and Dad, this helps the parents maintain their children's respect. This is good for your grandchildren and for you: they will respect you, too.

- **Do** *give your grandchildren a very clear message about education.* Tell them how important school and learning are. Ask your grandchildren about their grades and how they're doing, but even more important, ask them about what they're learning in school. Your interest in their learning encourages their interest in their learning.

  Here are the **Don'ts**:

- **Don't** *spoil your grandchildren by giving them too many material possessions.* It makes grandparents feel good to give, but it's not good for children to be given too much. They don't appreciate what they have and only want more. Each time you walk in the door, they expect gifts.
- **Don't** *sabotage your grandchildren's parents.* Don't secretly tell the children, for example, "Well, Dad is punishing you, but now that your dad is gone, I'll let you watch TV even though he said you couldn't." Sabotaging parents is the most damaging thing that grandparents can do. Gifted children often believe that they're equal to adults, and siding with them against their parents is likely to encourage opposition and rebelliousness.
- **Don't** *impose your value system on your children.* There may be differences in philosophy between a grandparent and a parent, but the grandparent must defer to the parent's wishes. Grandparents should share some (not too much) information based on their many years of parenting but must leave it up to the parents whether they wish to follow the advice. Sometimes giving your children a parenting book, newspaper article, or a tape works best, but again, giving your children too many newspaper clippings may only make them angry and cause them to feel like you're trying to control them.
- **Don't** *do too much for your grandchildren.* Encourage their independence.

- ***Don't*** *tell grandchildren that they're your favorites.* Don't say they're the smartest, the most creative, the best, or the most special. This may make them feel good, but another grandchild may learn about this message, too. By comparison, the other children will feel less favored. Don't call them "kings" or "princesses." They internalize these words as pressures and expectations and may expect too much of themselves or become dependent on praise and attention.

- ***Don't*** *talk to your grandchildren's parents about them in negative ways when the children might overhear* (referential speaking). Grandparents and parents may say, "He's just a mess," "She's so disorganized," "He's so shy," or "She's afraid to do anything," and the child may hear this and feel negatively labeled. It's always better to talk positively, but avoid the extremes.

Not all children are blessed with grandparents, nor are all adults of appropriate age fortunate enough to have grandchildren. Informally adopting a grandparent or grandchild may be a way to form a wonderfully warm substitute relationship that provides special joy for children and seniors alike.

8

AUNTS, UNCLES, AND COUSINS

Some children are not only blessed with parents and grandparents who love them but also have favorite aunts or uncles who adore them. Sometimes aunts or uncles don't have children of their own and may build an especially close relationship with their nieces or nephews. You may wonder what the pleasures and pitfalls of such special relationships may be.

For aunts or uncles without children, relationships with nieces and nephews permit them to experience a kind of fulfillment in a segment of their own lives that they might not otherwise experience. At holiday times, birthdays, and even on special trips, these aunts and uncles may enjoy the companionship of a niece or nephew whom they love and who loves them. For some, however, the joys are mixed blessings because the children may also be reminders that they will not or cannot ever have children of their own. For others, the blessings are only mixed with the relief that they chose not to have the responsibility or burden of parenting. The fun of being with their nieces or nephews only confirms for them that they've made the correct decision. As parents, let your siblings who don't have their own children choose whether to take an interest in your children.

What are the pleasures of these special aunt or uncle relationships? Sometimes aunts and uncles without children of their own can give your children learning experiences, fun excursions, and even gifts that you may not have time or money enough to afford. Because you know that your sisters or brothers are enjoying your children and that your children are benefiting from this special opportunity, you can be pleased for them as well as for your children. Some aunts and uncles are wonderful role models for nieces and nephews and share special skills or interests with them. If you are a single parent and you have a sister or brother of the same gender as your child (not your gender), it is even more important that your child has an appropriate same-gender role model. An uncle or aunt may be ideal.

There are also risks of special aunt and uncle relationships. Suppose your own sister or brother leads a lifestyle to which you would not like your children to be exposed, or what happens if your children complain to an aunt or uncle about how hard you are on them and she or he agrees with the children, taking their side against you? These are major problems for you and your children because you are likely to feel torn between wanting to be a good sister or brother and a good parent. You want to be a good sister or brother, but most important, you want to keep the power to guide your children's lives.

Here's the hard part! You should be firm and assertive if, and only if, Auntie or Uncle is a bad role model for your children or if she or he interferes with your discipline of your children. Here are some suggestions:

- Keep visits between your children and their aunts and uncles brief and impersonal.
- Don't allow long trips or large gifts.
- Communicate to aunts or uncles the changes you expect of them if they want to stay close to your children.
- Be firm. These are your children. Don't let anyone make you feel guilty about these difficult decisions.

If your sisters and brothers have their own children, they are less likely to take sides with your children against you and are also less likely to have time to build a special or individual relationship with your children. However, cousin rivalry can become a problem.

Many concerns discussed in Key 6 apply to relationships with cousins. Most important, parents must be sensitive about not acting out their own sibling rivalry through their children. Bragging about your children's giftedness does nothing to endear your siblings to you, nor does it encourage cousins to love each other. Calling one cousin the "smart" one and the other the "jock" causes serious problems for both. Although most parents know how inappropriate competitive comments can be, hardly any parents seem to be able to contain their enthusiasm about their gifted children's accomplishments. Conversations about your nieces' and nephews' successes are more empathic and sensitive than continuous announcements about your own children's awards and accomplishments.

For the most part, relationships with aunts, uncles, and cousins are wonderful connections for your children. If high risks aren't evident, consider your children fortunate to have these special extended family members.

9

^^

SINGLE PARENTING
AND DIVORCE

T he special challenges of parenting gifted children during and after divorce are intensified because gifted children's heightened sensitivities and extended perceptiveness make them even more vulnerable to the risks that attend single parenting. Children in single-parent homes, however, are no longer unique because more than half of the children in our society spend part of their childhoods in single-parent households.

Being a single parent because of divorce, death, or choice continues to be a somewhat lonely responsibility. One advantage of parenting alone, however, is that you may find that you can spend more social time with your children, and their good company can actually relieve some of the loneliness you may feel. Gifted children can become delightful partners for visits to concerts, museums, and resorts. Because of their high-level intellectual or artistic ability (or both), you may thoroughly enjoy exchanges of observations and conversations that are sometimes as stimulating and interesting as those with many adults. However, it is in this specific advantage that there is also risk.

Children who are such good company become easy to take along to adult activities. You may frequently invite them to join you, especially if you lack a significant other and also because of the guilt and expense that accompany leaving them alone with a sitter. Although taking your children along with you may expose them to advanced cultural opportunities that will surely do them no harm, it also exposes them to social and conversational opportunities with adults. Their adult social skills may further tempt you to include them. Even though your children may be easily accepted as adults and as parent partners at adult functions, their adult mannerisms may be oddly out of place when they are generalized to peer social situations. Furthermore, when you attempt to set limits, your adolescents may remind you of their vast experience and insist that you have no right to treat them in so childish a fashion. If you later choose not to include them in attractive adult activities, they may even question your right to leave them at home.

As adolescents who have been given adult status too soon, they may expect you to consult with them before you decide to date others and may voice their criticism of your friends of either gender. They've heard other adults criticize; they may consider it their equal right to do the same. Actually, after being "adultized" for so long, they may even object to being barred from adult conversations. Your teenagers, who used to fit in so well, begin to seem very out of place. You'll wonder why and how this negative transition has taken place. It is because adolescents are not prepared to be treated as children after they've become accustomed to being considered adults.

Now that you're conscious of the risks, you can more easily avoid the problems. From the start, keep a separate adult life for yourself. Join friends for an evening or two a week, and very specifically leave your children at home with trusted caretakers. You need not feel guilty: this is healthy for them. Don't confide intimate details to your children about other adults or a former spouse. The intimacy causes the children to feel close to you but elevates them beyond their levels of maturity. Try to share holidays and celebrations as a family with other families.

Don't tell your children that you will always love them more than anyone or share your bed with them (except during thunderstorms or for weekend morning fun). When you find another adult friend with whom you may choose to share your life, your children will feel betrayed, rejected, and angry at you and your friend. Your children can't be substitutes for your adult partner, no matter how needy and lonely you feel.

Finally, if you are a single mother, try to find appropriate male role models for your children, while recognizing that you're the most important role model for them. If you're a single dad, you'll want to find appropriate female role models.

If you're a single parent because of the death of your spouse, after the grieving period has eased, be sure to share stories with your children about their deceased parent—as spouse, as a child, and as an adult. Even a parent who is no longer living can be an excellent role model for children. Describe your spouse as a good role model, but give your children a balanced description. Your children don't require an image of their deceased parent as having been better than life. Emphasize the positive attributes of the deceased parent, but also let your children know that parents aren't perfect.

Divorce may have brought you to single parenthood, or you may be wondering how to explain to your gifted children that you and your spouse are contemplating divorce. If the latter is the case, it's likely that your children have been anxious about your marital problems for quite awhile, although occasionally children assume that all marriages are in constant conflict and don't anticipate a breakup.

If possible, it is good for both parents to share information about the breakup with their children together. Doing so usually avoids the "blame Mom–blame Dad" game. It's healthier for your children if you can remain respectful with each other even during the divorce process and despite the bitterness that both of you may feel. Give your children specific permission to love both parents.

Divorce isn't always as easy as we would like. Marriages often break up with outlandish and irrational behavior on the part of one or both spouses. Gifted children question morality issues and may feel a responsibility to mediate the relationship or take sides with one parent or the other. There may be almost no way you can prevent a furious adolescent from "snooping" into your adult relationships or lecturing to you or your former spouse about adultery. If you as a parent feel rejected, it is difficult not to encourage your children to see your side of a horrible mess. Children do not need to know all the details of your distressed adult lives. Even if they're gifted and seem to perceive and grasp it all, tell them you can't and won't share your adult issues with them. Of course, you need support for your loneliness and tears; however, counselors, close friends, and sometimes your own parents are your best support. Divorce is an enormous burden that should not be placed on the shoulders of adult-sounding children.

After the mess is over, try to move on to a better life. Don't remind your children when you're angry that their worst characteristics were inherited from the other parent. This causes them to feel helpless to change and angry at you because of the comparison to someone you no longer love.

When you arrange visitation, try to keep school rituals and routines regular for children, although admittedly, children adjust to some very strange visitation arrangements. Arrange for clear communication from schools, teachers, doctors, and activity coaches. Schools and churches usually understand their responsibilities for dual communication, provided you make such a request. Keep your children actively involved in interesting activities.

If your children come to visit you and are angry about the adjustment of having to leave the other home, it can make your alliance with them stronger if you say something nice about the parent they've just left. If you're negative about the other parent, they'll probably agree but will feel caught in the middle, and transferring from home to home will be brutal. If you can't avoid being angry with your former spouse when you exchange children, don't talk. Write polite notes instead.

Time and patience will help you and your children adjust to the traumas of divorce and/or single parenthood. Key 10 will help you to introduce your children to new relationships in a blended family if and when this situation arises.

10

BLENDING FAMILIES

Many gifted children spend part of their childhoods in single-parent families, or they join other families to form new family units. When this occurs, the new stepparents become important, and stepsiblings, stepgrandparents, and cousins become part of a new kinship circle.

Some of the adjustments discussed in this key apply to all children whether or not they're gifted. However, particular stepsibling combinations or grandparent relationships may cause some special problems for gifted children.

Parenting issues are first priority. It is too easy for the fun of blending to dissipate into a "my children–your children" brouhaha. Parents need to share their discipline guidelines before they move in together. Compromises and modifications can proceed more smoothly if the birth parent is the enforcer. The stepparent initially is accepted better in a friendly alliance. Children and adolescents are also much more accepting of a stepparent if they had not been given adult power or intimacy earlier. Parents need to stay united even though it is very tempting to rescue your own child from a stepparent's ire, which may cause the stepparent to become the "ogre" and frustrate you and your partner (see Key 3).

Before the new marriage takes place, prospective parents must discuss with each other their children's personalities, interests, and problems so that they can begin their new families with insights that prevent the unfortunate trespassing on sensitive feelings that can take place early in the new family. The solutions may be as simple as avoiding comments about diet and weight or as complex as understanding that each parent's oldest child has, for example, extraordinary musical talent. What could become a pleasant cooperative venture can easily erode to impossible competition. A child who has a reputation in the family for being best in an arena may experience a difficult personality crisis when another child coming into the family clearly excels in the same talent area. Parents and grandparents all need to make adjustments, but most of all, this is difficult for that child.

The competitiveness between two talented children may easily turn to anger and frustration if both children consider themselves equally talented in music, when in fact one is much more talented than the other. More worrisome than the anger is the depression that can occur for the less talented child, possibly even causing the less talented child to give up music altogether. This shutdown can be thought of as a "dethroning" process, whether it relates to having the most musical talent, intellectual capability, athletic skill, beauty, or creativity.

The approach to dealing with this issue of competition is similar to that described in Key 6. Parents must be *fair* but shouldn't treat children exactly the same. The children's specific talents should be enriched to the extent possible for each child. However, fair but not equal feels unfair to children who are accustomed to first place. They thus need to be handled gingerly. Explain to your children that competition should stay outside the family and that within the family all children can be talented, even if not equally capable. Remind them that it's normal to have competitive feelings, however. The "whole smart family" can exist even within a blended family. Be prepared to be patient, sensitive, and encouraging. Children require time and understanding for the difficult adjustment of blending families.

As in intact families, when children are closer in age and of the same gender, the competition is likely to be worse. Children may become incredibly angry when they have to share a parent or their "own" room with another sibling. They may also feel guilty about their unwillingness to share when kindness and sensitivity have been an integral part of their personalities in the past. If you don't introduce opportunities to talk about these issues, be prepared for some notable explosions of temper. Sometimes children who are close in age and interests actually enjoy the new close companionship so much that the competition is secondary. Be prepared for either event.

The children's other parents who are outside the new blended family are also critically important to successful blending and yet are hardly ever in control of their children's new family, and vice versa. It is terribly difficult for mothers or fathers to see their own children relating to another mother or father figure. It is almost as difficult for these parents to see their talented children become only second best in the other family. It exacerbates the pain when they themselves have not found another partner and observe the children enjoying their new united family unit while the old family feels painfully empty. Because both parents hardly ever marry and form blended families at the same time, the best way to encourage these parents to be supportive of the blending is to help them realize that they, too, will want support for blending if and when they remarry. It is also true that children adjust much better to blending families when all parents involved in the process are supportive.

The blending of families hardly ever begins smoothly, but with time and patience, many stepchildren learn to love and respect their stepparents (and vice versa), and many stepsiblings actually become close friends.

11

‚‚

EARLY CHILDHOOD TESTING

You think your child is gifted, but you're not really sure. Research indicates that parents' perceptions of their preschool children's giftedness are usually accurate; however, you may not have confidence in your perceptions.

You've observed your friends' children: sometimes they seem as capable as your child, and sometimes those comparisons make your son or daughter seem unusually intelligent. Of course, you really prefer not making comparisons, but they happen anyway.

You've heard people say that all parents think their children are gifted, so you're wondering if your love, commitment, and joy in your children's accomplishments are magnifying your appraisal of their capabilities. Although you've read about child development and have observed other children of similar age, the feelings you have continue to be ambiguous. Because you don't want to omit appropriate stimulating environments from your children's initiation into school, you're considering whether your child should be tested by a psychologist.

Tests can supply you with important information about your child's intellectual giftedness, as long as you recognize that test results tend to be somewhat unreliable for preschool children. Scores can easily be lowered by shyness, a bad day, or merely fear of a particular tester. Lucky guesses can enhance the score a little, but slightly higher scores cause fewer problems than dramatically lowered scores.

Here are several very good reasons for having your preschool child tested:

1. Children who are intellectually gifted may benefit from early entrance to kindergarten, special curriculum planning within kindergarten, or a uniquely enriched preschool environment.
2. Test scores give quantitative data, which you may or may not choose to share with the school when communicating about your child's special needs. These quantitative data are usually normative, which permits you to compare your child's development to that of a sample of average children of similar age.
3. Weak areas may be discovered that may be masked by your child's intellectual giftedness. Preschool testing permits you to assist your child in practicing these skills.
4. Test scores give you confidence in your personal observations or correct them appropriately. They can prevent you from placing too much pressure on your child.
5. Early test scores provide baseline information for monitoring your child's intellectual growth and progress.

Now that you've decided there may be a reason to test your child, you'll want to know where to find a tester. If you're determining whether your child should be entered into school early or if you believe your child may require special programming, you can request that your local school psychologist do the testing. If gifted children are not considered within the domain of the school psychologist, you must find a private psychologist or university psychological center familiar with testing gifted children. There's reason to emphasize that the psychologist be familiar with the specialty of gifted children; not all psychologists are. Don't hesitate to ask. The director of gifted education in your state's department of education may be able to help you to find an appropriate tester.

There are two individually administered IQ tests that are appropriate for testing preschool gifted children. The Wechsler Preschool and Primary Scale of Intelligence–Revised (WPPSI-R) provides both verbal and performance scores, and it is helpful to have both. Its disadvantage is that the scale may not go high enough for some very gifted children. The Stanford-Binet Intelligence Scale, Form L-M is mainly a verbal test with a more extensive scale. This test is recommended if your child exceeds the limits of the first test.

The Stanford-Binet, L-M has been updated with the Stanford-Binet IV; however, the more recent test is not useful for gifted children. Not only are children's scores much lower on the new test, but the scores do not discriminate well between children in the superior range and those in the very superior range. Apparently, recent test creators don't seem to see a need for discriminating among gifted children's abilities. Unfortunately, updated tests of intellectual abilities that could best guide you in planning for very gifted children are simply not available. However, psychologists who specialize in working with gifted children are aware of this testing dilemma and understand your special request for the older test.

If your child is already reading and doing math calculations, an achievement test is also appropriate. The test should be given orally in a one-to-one setting to attain the most accurate results. Developmental delays in small muscle coordination or immaturity may confound and lower the results of a written test for young children. A fair number of suitable tests are available that are relatively brief and provide reading and math information for a preschooler who may be demonstrating skills typical of school-age children.

Age four is usually early enough for a first testing if you require the information for school decision making. Because gifted children learn so rapidly, there may be a need for further achievement testing just before school entrance for academic placement. There is no further requirement for IQ testing for three or four years unless test results don't seem to match teacher or parent observations.

Prekindergarten screenings conducted by schools are not intended to assess giftedness. Although they provide the school with some important developmental information, they cannot be used to measure the extent of children's intellectual giftedness or academic achievement because the difficulty of the test items is not likely to be sufficient.

If you sense that your child is gifted but there are no early entrance decisions or specific curriculum changes that need to be considered, it's probably better to postpone testing until first grade, when scores become more reliable. Many gifted children learn to read only at the typical age in first grade, and for these children, individual psychoeducational testing can wait until school age.

12

‸‸‸

SELECTING A PRESCHOOL

In many ways the criteria for selecting a school for your gifted preschooler are identical to those for any child. There are only a few special considerations, and these are shared as final criteria to consider.

You may be looking for day care as a requirement for continuing your careers, or you may be looking only for part-time opportunities for your children. The criteria are surprisingly similar except that consistency and communication between home and school are even more critical if your children spend more of their day away from home. Communication between school and home is important not only because you will feel more secure about the environment being provided for your children, but also because you, as parents, can share in your children's developmental milestones despite your not being available to witness them at all times. A daily journal exchange can facilitate this communication. Your child care providers can be asked to document your children's daily accomplishments. They are likely to understand how important this is for you. Here are other criteria for you to consider:

- *Warm positive atmosphere.* Your visit to the preschool setting should provide you with a sense that the child care providers are loving toward all the children. If staff members seem to be targeting children who are troublemakers in their conversations with others, consider that your child could become one of those children, and this would not be a good school start. If instead they emphasize more positive approaches to problem solving, this augers well for their approach.

- *Stability of staff.* Stability of staff helps the consistency of programming. Schools that have a history of continuous staff turnover may not be selecting staff well or not training them sufficiently. It is also possible that the leadership of the school is inadequate. Obviously, occasional changes in staff are normal. You can best obtain this information from other parents whose children have been attending the school for awhile. If teachers have left with frequency, you may also want to ask about the reason.

- *Classroom organization and control.* A too orderly preschool can be stifling to children, but reasonable organization and limit setting are critical to a child's early learning of responsibility and self-discipline. Routines that teach children good manners, cleanup responsibilities, consideration for others, and respect for teachers provide good preparation for school and life. Disorganized, out of control class environments may cause feelings of insecurity for preschool children. Gifted children may be especially sensitive to the disorder.

- *Opportunities for creative expression and curiosity.* Toys and equipment should include painting and drawing supplies, small and large building blocks, and pretend and imaginative toys, as well as sturdy outdoor equipment. Opportunities go beyond equipment. An atmosphere in which children are expected to explore, create and invent, and feel and touch, rather than copy adult direction and fill in lines or work pages, underscores a creative environment. Find out if children are encouraged to question by observing in the classroom. If the structure is too rigid, children learn to follow but their curiosity is stifled.

- *Fostering the love of books.* Almost every day care center or preschool fosters the love of literature, reading, and drama. Yet this cannot be overlooked as a criterion because the love of books is a prerequisite to the love of learning. Several story hours a day should not be replaced by a convenient television set, and television should either make up a very small part of children's learning in preschool or not be present at all.

- *Music, dance, and movement.* Creative movement provides opportunities for the development of children's love of music and rhythm. Dance or some form of movement to music should be part of almost every preschool day. Skipping, hopping, jumping, and marching to music are appropriate examples. Many schools elaborate far beyond these basics.

- *Outdoor play and exploration.* The exploration of nature may be limited at urban centers, but learning about weather, animals, and nature can be carried out in parks and playgrounds and is as critical to gifted children as learning from books. Observation skills and curiosity are encouraged by an awareness of the outdoors, as are sensitivity to animal families and relationships between people and nature.

- *Value systems.* Religious points of view and values about honesty, respect, animal life, conservation, and so on, should be a reasonable match with your family values. Although they need not be identical, they should at least complement what you believe is appropriate for your children.

- *Freedom to choose within limitations.* Some school curricula are the same for the entire class, and others permit children to make all the choices for activities. Neither extreme is productive for gifted children in the long run. Rigid preschool lessons do not tap individual giftedness because all children are likely to be working on similar skills;

therefore, rigid lessons do not provide challenges for your gifted child. Allowing the children to make all the choices is also risky. Gifted children are likely to select their areas of interest and pursue them but may ignore or neglect some of the more boring skills they may require for kindergarten. Furthermore, a school that permits children to make all the choices empowers preschoolers too much. The children may assume school will always be that way and balk at later school environments that feel restrictive by comparison.

- *Academic preparation.* Preschools should provide some academic preparation, but not too much. Gifted children often express a thirst for academic learning that tempts parents and teachers to provide more and more. Some gifted four year olds may wish to read or do math all day, and for those who show readiness, a little time each day is appropriate. A more holistic approach is as important for gifted children as it is for all children. It is not appropriate that any child's self-esteem be based only on the child's capacity to learn.

- *Recognition of giftedness.* The staff of an excellent preschool shouldn't feel threatened by a parent's discussion of a child's gifted abilities. If a teacher rapidly changes the subject or responds that all the children in the school are gifted, this teacher is not likely to be responsive to your gifted child's individual needs. A response that recognizes individual differences and refers to some other children's special needs as well can reassure you that you are in an environment that values your child's unique creative and learning abilities in a balanced way.

Firsthand observations of a preschool class in session using a checklist and taking notes will help you to evaluate these criteria and some of your own. An interview with the teacher and telephone calls to other parents will assist you in gathering other information.

47

If you are having difficulty in choosing between schools, rate each criterion on a one to five scale and add up your final score. Don't let the numbers make your final decision for you, but permit them to influence your decision making in a more concrete way. You may feel disappointed when you find that few preschools satisfy all your criteria. This is only the beginning of realism as it relates to future school selections. Schools can hardly ever afford to be perfect, so you'll need to have realistic standards. Many fine schools are available.

13

WHEN TO START KINDERGARTEN

D ates for kindergarten entrance are established based on the developmental readiness typical of most five year olds. It is logical to have a specific date, and it is just as logical to provide a basis for exceptions. Although some states allow exceptions based on testing, other states permit no departures from the deadline date. Even within states, school districts may have a variety of entrance dates, rules, and variations thereof.

In some places, it is considered fashionable to delay children's entrance to kindergarten, especially boys. Parents and teachers often expect that an extra year of maturity will make it more likely that these children will become "best" students and leaders in their classes. Teachers often remind parents that this also improves their competitive sports performance and their confidence. Although there don't appear to be data on their improved sports performance or their confidence, there are data on achievement, and research has not borne out what appeared to many parents and teachers to be intuitively true and common sense. Findings indicate that children who are held back from entering kindergarten do not do as well academically on the average as children who are entered in a timely manner. Furthermore, in some school districts, so many children are held back that indeed the average age of kindergarten children is similar to what it used to be for first graders. Because of this, kindergarten teachers have often felt pressured to design a first-grade curriculum.

Research findings are based on populations, and although they are helpful in guiding decision making, you'll want a professional individual assessment before you make a final decision. School or private psychologists who specialize in working with gifted children can evaluate your child's school readiness.

If your child's tests are in the very superior IQ range, your child may be better off being young in the class. Research in the field of gifted education continuously finds that children who are accelerated or entered early achieve better with the additional challenge. Socially, they adjust as well as gifted children of typical kindergarten entrance age who have not been entered early or accelerated.

Girls tend to mature earlier than boys. Although children are sometimes actually less mature than their classmates, at other times, symptoms of immaturity are indicative that a child has not been given enough independence. These same symptoms may also mean a child has been given too much power and has not learned to respect adult leadership. Thus, symptoms of immaturity may merely represent inappropriate behaviors that can be changed.

Some teachers may assume that shy children are immature when their shyness may actually be related to their temperament or their lack of group experience. Entering school in a timely way will increase social experience and may actually facilitate maturity. If your child has a shy temperament, she may nevertheless be very capable and shouldn't be penalized for a quiet personality. By preventing a shy child from experiencing kindergarten in a timely manner, you may actually be hurting confidence by encouraging the child's hesitancy.

There is almost no good reason to prevent intellectually gifted children from entering school at the age suggested for entrance unless they have verified learning disabilities. If the school offers optional early entrance, intellectual and academic assessments provide your best objective guides. If your children are tall, this may help you to feel more comfortable about early entrance even though there is no research indicating that height makes a difference in either intellectual or social adjustment. If sports that require height are your first priority, this may cause you some hesitancy about early entrance. However, if you base your decision on sports capability, this indicates to your children that your first school priority is not academic, so don't be surprised if your children value sports more than learning.

A decision for your child must be made individually and carefully. Such subjective factors as differing opinions between the child's parents, the classroom makeup of a particular school, and the age of siblings are additional subtleties that influence your decision making. Although surely all these issues require some consideration, the dominant decision maker that is frequently heard, but is inappropriate, is the parent's wish that the child be at the top of the class academically. Actually, this is a very competitive wish that can doom your child to underachievement. Because the child is unlikely to be challenged for the first few years and will excel easily, when challenge comes along, your child is likely to be unaccustomed to study and perseverance. The fear of disappointing parents and self at not being at the top inhibits the child from taking the risk of working hard. It's easier for the child to blame teachers or boredom than to question the pressure he or she feels at no longer being smartest in the class.

If your child is younger than others in the class, consider the future advantage if your child is not working as hard as expected. You can explain that he or she will have to work a little harder to keep up with children who are a little older. If your child is oldest by far and intellectually gifted as well, parents may find it a bit harder to find encouraging words when school grades drop.

Intellectually gifted children, like all children who enter kindergarten, should have opportunities for learning new academic material. For some gifted children, this requires early entrance to kindergarten. For many, the typical entrance age is suitable. For hardly any child is it appropriate to wait an extra year.

14

∿∿

ENHANCING LEARNING IN THE FAMILY

P arents can experience the joy of enhancing their children's learning in many shared ways, beginning with encouraging a love of reading and including an appreciation of culture, the arts, the environment, exploration, science, government, and the world community. The list goes on, and information in this key includes only a minimum of suggestions. Additional Reading at the end of the book lists numerous books to help you to expand your children's learning. Libraries and bookstores can provide many more.

Your home provides the first learning laboratory. Kitchen science and cooking are effective teaching tools. Encyclopedias, atlases, and globes help to expand your children's horizons and their love of geography beyond the living room. Play dough, water colors, sand boxes, and clay permit creative exploration of the arts. A piano or guitar being played by an amateur musician-parent becomes the basis for many sing-alongs and play-alongs. Stores abound with records and tapes, and listening to taped stories (without visuals) encourages children's listening skills. Dancing to recorded music facilitates your children's coordination and their love of music. When parents join in the dance, families become less inhibited. Add ballet slippers to your dance performances, and even the awkward feel graceful.

Be sure to explore your community resources. Art museums, parks, conservatories, museums of natural history,

53

aquariums, observatories, nature centers, children's museums, theaters, and concert halls may be closer than you realize.

Trips or visits outside your community increase in value if your children are involved in the planning. Learning how to send for brochures, maps, and travel information is a good skill for children to develop. Trips become more interesting for them if they can participate in planning the routes and places to visit.

Cameras and tape recorders increase the depth of learning when children travel and preserve the memories and knowledge they obtain. A microcassette tape recorder is much less cumbersome than a video camera and can serve as an oral journal for a child as well as an interviewing tool for friends they meet along the way. Interviewing a forest ranger on tape may forever preserve messages about conservation, and your children will remember them better through the personalization, involvement, and repetition.

When you can tie travel or community activities to your children's school learning, this adds relevance to what school contributes. Farms are wonderful exploration areas for urban and suburban children. Seeing sugarcane being grown in Louisiana or corn in Iowa makes a memorized list of products much more meaningful. Talking to growers or farmers about their problems and recording the conversations on tape provides special insights for your children and their classmates. Cities are also important for all to visit and learn about. Remember that talking with different people adds depth to every visit.

History comes alive with a visit to a great-grandparent's home or a home for senior citizens. Social histories based on questions planned together are exciting for your children, for you, and for the elderly.

There may be the risk of overwhelming your children with too much culture. If you're enthusiastic and they're uninterested, this may be a signal for you either to slow down or to do some adult activities without them.

If there are two parents in the family, it's important to preserve positive united interest. Unfortunately, if one parent voices dislike for the ballet or art, some children are likely to fight exploring those cultural experiences. The key seems to be to develop genuine interests and enthusiasm and to avoid overdoing.

Although schools invest the most time into teaching your children skills, parents truly are their most important teachers. If you can avoid placing pressure on your children and recognize that overload can cause disinterest, your modeling of a love of life and learning will provide the very best of opportunities for your children.

15

~~~~~~

LEARNING TO LOVE READING

Gifted children often anticipate with excitement the opportunity to learn to read and enthusiastically share their first conquests of the written word with their parents and teachers. Some gifted children learn to read as early as age two years, but others don't read until they're taught in first grade. Enthusiasm about the preschool child's early reading can be positive and encouraging, but parents should be careful not to exhibit their children's early reading by bragging about them or urging them to read aloud to all visitors. There's the risk that their children will read only for attention instead of for the intrinsic love of the books and stories.

For those students who love reading, school is very likely to be a positive experience. Some gifted children struggle with learning to read, however, and the educational process becomes more difficult. Because good reading skill is often equated with intelligence, these children may lose confidence quickly. Following are suggestions for general encouragement of the love of reading for all children, along with special recommendations for gifted children who have reading problems. The latter recommendations can help you to guide children who cope with reading problems toward self-confidence and independence despite their reading struggles.

- Family reading should begin in infancy and extend throughout life. There are no grade or age limits at which family reading should stop. Reading together aloud or silently creates an atmosphere for children to love books.

- Permit children to stay up half an hour later at night if they're in their beds reading to themselves (children don't usually like to sleep; it's adults who do).

- Encourage children to read whatever they like during this time before going to sleep. Don't insist they read grade-level material. Comics, cartoons, sports magazines, easy material, and books read many times are all good for reading enjoyment. If they love reading, they can expand their interests as their reading improves.

- Model reading by keeping books, newspapers, and magazines around that your children see you enjoy.

- Become a regular visitor with your children to public libraries. Encourage them to attend story hours at an early age, and when they're old enough to ride to the library on their bikes, encourage their regular visits. Wander through public libraries in new cities as part of your travel plan and encouragement of curiosity.

- When shopping in malls or on main streets, stop by bookstores and browse or even purchase books. Encourage your children to choose books they'll read and later cherish.

- Monitor TV watching, and limit video games. If this becomes a power struggle, you may find using a plug lock* very effective. Too much TV takes time away from reading.

Intellectually gifted children are usually excellent readers, but some are not strong readers and may even have reading disabilities. Disabilities can produce anxieties for all children, but for gifted children, the disparity between their thinking abilities and their reading capabilities can cause considerable frustration or embarrassment. Here are some suggestions to follow should you observe a reading problem:

*For more information about plug locks, please call 1 (800) 475-1118.

- Ask your school psychologist or private clinic to provide an evaluation for a reading disability.
- If this yields no explanation, you may want to have your child evaluated for a specific reading disability called *scotopic sensitivity syndrome.** This is a biological disorder that is typically inherited. Thus, a parent or an aunt or uncle is likely to have a history of an early reading problem. Scotopic sensitivity syndrome is helped dramatically by colored lenses. Different colors seem to work for different people.
- Don't force your children to read aloud at home because you may unintentionally convey anxiety about your children's reading to them. Most parents feel tense when poor readers read aloud to them. As adult readers, they rarely find oral reading important. Children should read aloud if they choose to do so, though.
- Encourage children to read to their younger siblings, provided these siblings aren't better readers than they are. They shouldn't do this in your presence but alone with their sisters or brothers.
- Ask your children's teachers to permit them to read aloud to preschool or kindergarten children. The books are easy, and the simplicity of the reading and the enthusiastic reception from small children build poor readers' confidence and their love of reading.
- Encourage children to read stories while listening to tapes of the stories. Don't hover over them to be sure they're actually reading; eventually they will.
- Don't read homework instructions to your children. Encourage them to read the instructions to themselves several times. Also suggest that they "whisper" read them (reading in a whispered voice to oneself). This helps them to concentrate and understand the instructions better. This seems to yield a great improvement in some children's comprehension.

*For more information about scotopic sensitivity syndrome, please call 1 (800) 475-1118.

- If your children continue to require assistance in under-standing assignments because of reading problems, tape record the instructions and let them listen while they're reading them. It is better to listen to the tape recorder than to become dependent on parent or teacher attention. They can stop the tape recorder, rewind it, and listen as many times as it takes for them to understand.

- Content area textbooks, such as social studies or science, should be made available to children on cassette tapes for simultaneous listening while reading. This is likely to increase their reading vocabulary as well as prevent feel-ings of inadequacy that arise from their lack of content knowledge.

- Don't assume poor readers are less intelligent because they don't read well.

- Don't force poor readers to read aloud under unpre-dictable or embarrassing circumstances.

- Don't unintentionally label poor readers negatively at home or school by talking about their problems (referen-tially) to other adults within their hearing.

- Don't take responsibility for poor readers because they can't read. Identify a means by which they can carry on activities independently using audio equipment or illus-trations rather than people. Continued one-to-one help only encourages dependence and makes them feel less intelligent.

- Encourage poor readers to become actively involved in drama and forensics. They may require a cassette recorder to help them prepare their presentations, but mastery of verbal material will help build their confidence.

- Be patient and supportive. If your children continue to read in an unpressured way, they may eventually master and learn to love reading. Many gifted adults have a histo-ry of early reading problems.

16

~~~~~~

SCHOOL IDENTIFICATION OF GIFTEDNESS

Your gifted children may have been identified for school programs to enhance and encourage their talents, or you may be confused because, indeed, one or more of your children have not been identified despite your belief in their need for special programming.

The first federal definition of giftedness that was used by schools as a basis for identification was included in a national report by Marland in 1972. It is important because it was the basis for legislation for the identification of giftedness in many states and is still used in many school districts:

> Gifted and talented children are those identified by professionally qualified persons who, by virtue of outstanding abilities, are capable of high performance. These are children who require differentiated educational programs and services beyond those normally provided by the regular school program in order to realize their contribution to self and society.
>
> Children capable of high performance include those with demonstrated achievement and/or potential in any of the following areas:

1. General intellectual ability
2. Specific academic aptitude
3. Creative or productive thinking
4. Leadership ability
5. Visual and performing arts
6. Psychomotor ability

Public Law 100-297 (1988) provided schools with the most current national definition of giftedness. This definition was recommended in the 1993 federal report, *National Excellence: A Case for Developing America's Talent* (Public Law 100-297, Sec. 4103. Definitions):

> The term "gifted and talented students" means children and youth who give evidence of high performance capability in areas such as intellectual, creative, artistic, or leadership capacity, or in specific academic fields, and who require services or activities not ordinarily provided by the school in order to fully develop such capabilities.

Another definition popularly used for gifted programming was developed by Joseph Renzulli at the University of Connecticut. He based his definition upon descriptions of creatively productive persons who make important contributions to society. His definition of gifted behavior is that which reflects an interaction among three basic clusters of human traits: above average general and/or specific ability, high levels of task commitment, and creativity. Children who possess or are capable of developing this composite set of traits and applying them to any potentially valuable area of human performance are defined by him as gifted.

Even if your children are gifted, your children's school may not be providing for their types of giftedness. Schools and states differ in their approaches to identifying children for gifted programming, and many do not even provide such programming. Furthermore, some schools may have programs that provide for only certain kinds of giftedness; for example, they may provide only for high achievers and neglect those children who possess leadership, creative, and artistic abilities. Intellectual giftedness is the most frequent type of giftedness for which schools provide, and even this may not be adequately provided for within your school district. Also, gifted underachievers and learning-disabled gifted students are not included in programs in many school districts, despite their special needs.

The percentages of students included in gifted programming vary significantly. The Marland definition of giftedness suggested a minimum of 3 to 5 percent of a school's population. Some school districts identify an arbitrary 5 percent. Other districts that boast of broader programs may include as many as 25 percent of their students in some kind of gifted programming. A recent report indicated that four states identified more than 10 percent of their student enrollment as gifted and talented, and twenty-one states identified fewer than 5 percent.

For many years, economically disadvantaged students and minority groups were greatly underserved, particularly when IQ score cutoffs were the main identification technique. More recently, efforts to identify and program for these populations appropriately have increased dramatically. Despite the improvement in identification, Native American, African-American, and Hispanic populations are often under-identified and underserved.

Some school districts use only group IQ scores for identification of their students. Other schools may include creativity tests, student products (such as artwork or music), peer or parent nominations, and/or teacher recommendations. The identification process may seem quite confusing to parents, and this key cannot be effective in clarifying every school's rationale for their identification methods of gifted children. However, parents shouldn't hesitate to ask questions of school personnel. Schools will undoubtedly be happy to communicate their philosophies and selection criteria.

IQ tests continue to be a priority test for use in identifying children's giftedness. The initials IQ stand for intelligence quotient. The term came from tests that were originally created by Alfred Binet in France in 1905; he used a chronological/mental age formula for the purpose of predicting whether children were sufficiently intelligent to benefit from schooling. IQ tests have been changed and revised many times since Binet's first tests, and educators have become much more sophisticated in their use. Although these tests are often still referred to as intelligence tests, they measure only some kinds of intelligence, and scores are affected by cultural environment and learning opportunities.

Despite the problems with IQ tests, they can still be used cautiously to predict how well children will do in various educational environments. IQ scores from group intelligence tests are typically used to identify gifted students because they continue to be administered regularly in most schools. Some of the better known group intelligence tests are the Cognitive Abilities Test, the Henmon-Nelson Test of Mental Ability, the SRA Primary Mental Abilities Tests, and the Otis-Lennon Mental Ability Test. Despite their comparatively low cost and convenient group administration, however, they have shortcomings. Group tests tend to be less reliable and less valid than individual tests. Also, children who are not motivated produce lower IQ scores than their apparent abilities indicate. Group tests are mainly verbal and dependent upon actual school achievement; therefore, they are biased against nonverbal gifted children or children who come from disadvantaged environments. Group tests tend to be unreliable at high IQ levels; a few chance errors may substantially lower a gifted student's IQ score. They are typically timed, and children who write or think slowly may be penalized. Despite the problems with group tests, children who score high on them are always capable and certainly should be included in gifted programs. However, other identification methods should be used for identifying unmotivated or culturally deprived students.

Some schools also administer individual IQ tests to gifted students. These must be administered by the school psychologist, and each administration takes approximately two hours. Because of the expense involved, most schools do not test entire populations but only students who pass a preliminary group screening or those who have special problems. These tests are discussed in Key 17.

Schools usually identify specific academic talent by using standardized achievement tests, such as the Iowa Tests of Basic Skills, the Metropolitan Achievement Tests, the SRA Achievement Series, the California Achievement Tests, or the California Test of Basic Skills. Two important problems should be considered relative to standardized achievement test scores. The first concerns the *grade-equivalent score.* Grade equivalent refers to the average score earned by children at a particular grade level on a particular test, not to the grade level at which a specific gifted child can function well in the classroom. Sometimes parents make the assumption that if gifted fourth graders perform well at the eighth-grade equivalent on math achievement tests, they can perform successfully at that grade level in the classroom. Although the children may be good math students, they probably lack many skills of average eighth graders and many more compared with gifted eighth graders. Grade-equivalent scores can be misleading and should be used only as indicators that students need special challenge. Further diagnostic testing should be used to determine the specific skills.

The second problem of standardized achievement test scores is related to the *low ceiling score* of typical achievement tests. Most achievement tests are not sufficiently difficult to measure the high abilities, knowledge, and skill levels of very able children. Many students score at the ceiling level or "top out" of the test. Thus, it is sometimes assumed that all these children are equally talented and need a similar skill development program. In fact, after diagnostic testing, or even with the use of more difficult achievement tests, a wide range of advanced skill levels is found among these children.

Creativity tests can be used to confirm a teacher's observations about the creativity of one or more students or to identify creative students whose talents are not obvious in the classroom. Creativity tests are far from perfect. Scores from a single creativity test may be quite misleading. A student who in fact does extraordinarily creative work in art or science can produce an average creativity score. Creativity is a complex ability that can take many forms. Data from creativity tests should be combined with observation to make decisions regarding creativity. Most schools that attempt to identify creativity use at least two forms of identification.

There are two main categories of creativity test: divergent thinking tests and inventories that assess personality and biographical traits. Divergent thinking tests require students to think of many answers to open-ended problems, such as giving unusual uses for a newspaper or brick or imagining the consequences of unlikely events. Divergent thinking tests are scored using such criteria as fluency (the number of ideas produced) and originality (uniqueness of the ideas). The Torrance Tests of Creative Thinking are the most widely used divergent thinking tests. The Structure of

Intellect Learning Abilities Tests by Mary Meeker also include divergent thinking tests, as well as tests of many other separate abilities.

The PRIDE, GIFT, GIFFI I, and GIFFI II instruments are inventories used to assess personality and biographical information. Such personality traits as curiosity, humor, and risk taking appear again and again in studies of creative, productive people.

Teacher checklists are also often used in the identification of creativity. Leadership characteristics are also typically identified by teacher checklists. Parent and peer questionnaires are sometimes used for the identification of all kinds of giftedness, but particularly the areas of creativity and leadership.

Identification for the visual and performing arts, if indeed schools provide such programs, are usually quite specific to the particular art form. Creativity tests have not been found to be effective for specific arts identification. Thus, artistic products, such as portfolios, are typically used for identification of the visual arts, and actual tryout performances are used for music or drama.

Very few general elementary or secondary public schools sponsor such programs for students talented in the visual and performing arts. Art and music teachers try to cultivate their students' special talents, but more frequently, students are advised to take private lessons outside school. Unfortunately, for economically disadvantaged students who may be talented in the visual and performing arts, outside teachers may simply not be a practical economical alternative. However, many large cities and some states provide magnet specialty schools in these areas.

17

▼▼▼

INDIVIDUAL
EVALUATIONS

M any parents are confused about whether to have their gifted children evaluated privately and, if so, when the testing should be done. Testing and evaluation considerations related to early childhood are discussed in Key 11. This key relates to specific evaluation concerns for school-age children.

Whether or not your children have been identified by the gifted identification system of your children's school, you may wish to have further individual evaluations conducted either by the school or by a private psychologist. If you want information for acceleration or enrichment considerations or if you believe your children are underachieving, further evaluation is appropriate. If you believe your children's school is not providing appropriately for your gifted children, individual testing can provide support for your assumptions or may verify that your children's needs are being met in the school program. Career preference testing may also be important for your teenage gifted children when they are multitalented and are confused about how they can direct their multiple talents toward future careers. Parents can request testing by the school psychologist even if such evaluation is not part of the school's usual identification procedures.

When schools do not include testing of gifted students as a psychological responsibility, you may need to search out private psychologists, although only a very small percentage of psychologists have backgrounds in the area of giftedness. University centers that have programs for gifted educators are likely also to have facilities for psychological assessment of gifted children.

School or private psychologists are likely to use one of several intelligence tests. The most frequently used series are the Wechsler Intelligence Scales, including a preschool test, a school-age test, and an adolescent/adult version. All individual tests are listed in Tests and Identification Instruments at the end of this book. The Wechsler tests provide a Verbal IQ score and a Performance (nonverbal) IQ score, along with the combined Full-Scale IQ score. The performance test is excellent for identifying spatial abilities that predict higher skills in mathematics and science.

Although the Wechsler tests are helpful for identifying strengths and weaknesses, it is possible to score only as high as 155 on these tests. This score can be achieved only if children are gifted in all areas. Furthermore, the new Wechsler (WISC) III seems to reflect scores that are, on the average, eight points lower than the older test on the gifted end of the scale. Thus, this commonly used test has some very real limitations for extremely gifted children despite its helpfulness in many other ways.

The 1986 Stanford-Binet Intelligence Scale–Fourth Edition is not recommended for gifted children because its scores are about 13.5 points lower than the older form L-M of the same test. The main problem is that the upper limit of the Fourth Edition is lower than that of the previous edition. Therefore, extraordinary intellectual talent (for example, an IQ of 175) can't be identified. If one uses the chronological/ mental age formula recommended by Alfred Binet in his original test, there is almost no ceiling for elementary children using Form L-M. By the teenage years, however, even form L-M has significant limitations for identifying highly gifted students. The test is simply not difficult enough for very gifted teenagers, nor is there an alternative identical psychological test that measures IQ scores above 155.

Individual achievement tests, including the Peabody Individual Achievement Test-R, the Woodcock-Johnson Achievement Test-R, and the Wide Range Achievement Test, are typically administered by psychologists. The last test involves writing, and there may be a disadvantage in using it for some children who may have difficulty with writing. The first two tests are oral and are less susceptible to handwriting problems.

If parents are concerned about their children's symptoms of stress, rebelliousness, or depression, they may request that a psychologist administer personality assessments or projective tests. The results from those assessments can be helpful in understanding pressures, power issues, or frustrations gifted children may feel.

Psychologists are trained to interpret for parents all cognitive and affective testing, and therefore, you should not hesitate to ask questions until you feel comfortable about understanding how to guide your children toward appropriate educational and vocational choices. Individual testing can be very important for making programming decisions for your children. Acceleration and grade-skipping decisions should not be made without the guidance of such detailed evaluations. Because evaluations for gifted children are typically related to mental health issues, rather than learning needs alone, health insurance sometimes provides partial payment for private evaluations.

There are a great many career tests that can be used for guiding gifted children toward higher education and decision making for their futures. The specific test is less critical than the counselor. It is important that the career counselor have an in-depth understanding of the many advanced careers available to very talented young adults. The issues of multiple talents and interests should be combined with the counselor's knowledge of actual opportunities for positions in a field. It is unwise to assume that gifted children should follow only their immediate interests if that career direction does not provide opportunity for complexity and growth. There is also the risk that gifted young people may invest 8 to 10 years in career preparation for an interesting career in which they will not be able to find employment. In addition to being guided by a knowledgeable counselor, students should take the initiative actually to interview people who are employed in the careers they may be considering.

If evaluations are interpreted by persons familiar with the special issues related to giftedness, you may be able to prevent some of the pitfalls and pressures that can affect your children by reason of their giftedness. Furthermore, the specialists who conduct the evaluation may be able to assist you in advocating for your gifted children's educational and psychological needs.

18

~~~~~~

SUBJECT ACCELERATION AND INDIVIDUALIZED INSTRUCTION

The awareness of actual lack of academic challenge for your gifted child is the initiating factor in the exploration of the use of any accelerative strategy. This may be brought to your attention by your child or your child's teacher. Gifted resource programs, classroom enrichment, and subject acceleration provide appropriate curriculum adjustments for most gifted children.

Although grade skipping is usually the preferred arrangement for students who have very high IQs and strong overall achievement, many gifted children excel in only one or two academic areas. These children are not good candidates for entire grade skips; however, they seem to thrive when a particular subject area is either compacted or skipped entirely.

Accelerated progression through a subject, or *acceleration,* can involve having children do all the basic work in a subject without doing as many examples or practice skills, thus accomplishing it in much less time. Skipping is preferred if tests indicate the child already shows competence in the subject and can therefore go on to the next grade in that particular subject. Acceleration in one or two subjects can be accomplished within the classroom, or students can actually move to the next grade for a subject skip.

Surprisingly, unlike grade skipping, subject skipping has not been well researched. Nevertheless, it is not only frequently accomplished but is often recommended by teachers. In contrast to the negative attitudes often exhibited toward grade skipping, many educators feel very comfortable about subject acceleration. Sometimes subject skipping is the only acceleration required for students who have a specific academic talent. Subject skipping can also be used experimentally as a step to grade skipping if parents and teachers are uncertain about how the student will adjust to a grade skip.

The decision for subject acceleration is much simpler than that for grade skipping. Although IQ tests may be used, they may not even be required. Individual achievement tests in reading, mathematics, science, spelling, or social studies, end-of-book tests, and class performance serve satisfactorily to indicate to educators and parents that students are already competent in most of the topics to be taught during the school year ahead. If the student demonstrates approximately 70 percent competence, it is certainly not logical to devote a year to teaching what this student could probably learn individually in a few days or weeks. Although it is important that missed skills be learned, a year devoted to this same curriculum would be counterproductive. Not only is it likely to be boring to the student, it gives the student the message that there is little to learn in school.

After the student demonstrates competence, the decision of how to challenge the student within a subject depends on such variables as school scheduling, teacher flexibility, other students in the class, the subject itself, and the child's age and temperament.

School scheduling that provides the same time block for a subject in two adjacent grades may facilitate sending a child into the next grade classroom for a subject. For example, the simplest curriculum adjustment for a first grader who has demonstrated math competence might be one in which the student is sent to the second-grade classroom down the hall at 10:15 each day for math. Concurrent subject scheduling is more likely to occur in primary than higher grades.

Sometimes attempts to send a child to the next grade result in so much disruption of the child's schedule that it seems wiser to adjust the curriculum within the classroom. This alternative requires teacher flexibility. The teacher is already working with a range of skills and abilities for the grade level in his or her classroom, and some teachers may not be willing to add yet another level beyond the grade he or she is teaching at present.

If there are other students in the class at a similar skill level, this facilitates either out-of-class or in-class acceleration. It is always easier for teachers to make exceptions in the curriculum when many students are involved. Also, most students enjoy being part of a small group and feel less isolated than if they are the only one sent to another class or doing special work.

The nature of the subject to be accelerated must also be considered in the curriculum adjustment. Such subjects as mathematics and spelling lend themselves to individualized curriculum, but much of reading, social studies, and science is enhanced by group discussion or interaction. Components of each of the latter subjects can also be individualized, but students may truly lose some important perspectives in these subjects if they study in isolation.

Last and most important is consideration of the age and temperament of the individual child. Younger children may feel more hesitant about leaving their classroom and joining another class. Shy children may find it more difficult than more socially comfortable children. Although none of these variables should preclude encouraging a child to risk the new experience, parents and teachers should be sensitive to signs of tension, which are indicators that the child is feeling stress. Initial tensions should be expected, however, and modifications should not be discontinued immediately. On the other hand, if the child continues to show signs of stress when joining another class or working alone, other alternatives should be explored.

Although some gifted children thrive with individualized instruction, others feel isolated and prefer class participation. It's important to recognize that children who work independently and seem content with an individualized curriculum continue to require feedback and interest from teachers. Sometimes teachers assume that gifted children require almost no teaching and interaction. Even though these assumptions are correct for a very limited number of students, most gifted students require the same encouragement and interest on which other students thrive. They simply need it at an accelerated pace and at a more in-depth level.

It is important to realize that when a gifted child does not achieve in an individualized curriculum, this is not an indicator that the child does not require challenge, only a symptom that the child requires an adjustment in teaching style.

19

‸‸‸

GRADE SKIPPING

For a small percentage of gifted children, skipping one or more grades may be the best approach to providing academic challenge. Parents and teachers often avoid making recommendations for grade skipping from concern that it places too much pressure on the children and that the skipping will negatively affect their social adjustment. Adults may want to remind themselves, however, that doing nothing is also making a decision. If they don't make accommodations to challenge their gifted children or students, this gives these children a message that academic challenge is a lesser priority than social conformity and that hard work is unimportant. This message of conformity may cause problems when children become adolescents. Teenagers may repeat the message in another form and tell their parents and teachers that social life is their main priority and that they don't want to work hard on their schoolwork.

Individual tests of academic ability (IQ) and achievement, discussed in Key 17, are the most important evaluative measures used for acceleration decision making. Despite the many documented problems of IQ tests, they provide good predictors for successful grade skipping.

The availability and quality of school enrichment programs and the academic makeup of the child's present class, as well as that of the class to which the child would be advanced, should also be considered. Peer academic environments can vary from grade to grade, and sometimes a challenging peer group in the lower grade can provide more appropriate learning than a less challenging peer group in the higher grade.

Other variables that should be considered are motivation or lack thereof, social adjustment, physical size and maturity, grades, and attitude of the receiving teacher. These are of lesser importance than test scores and academic environment because (1) grade skipping may improve motivation; (2) all studies indicate that grade skipping has no negative effect on social adjustment, and some research has shown that grade skipping actually helps adjustment; (3) physical size, maturity, and grades don't appear to make a difference in adjustment; and (4) although the attitude of the receiving teacher appears to make a dramatic, immediate difference, it does not seem to have long-term effects.

In reviewing the variables to be considered for grade skipping, it becomes clear that the most important criteria relate to an academically challenging environment, with all other variables of much lesser importance. It is also relatively clear that test scores are the best indicators for grade or subject skipping, despite their limitations.

You may wonder why it is that so many parents, teachers, and administrators oppose grade skipping when controlled research documents its success, both academically and socially (some research reviews of grade skipping are included in Additional Reading). People tend to base their evaluations of the success of grade skipping on their personal experience with children who were grade skipped. Almost everyone can recount a grade-skipping story about an adolescent who has experienced difficult social adjustment problems, and they are quick to assume that the problems were caused by the skipping of one or more grades. Normal adolescents, however, gifted or otherwise, skipped or not skipped, experience developmentally appropriate problems during adolescence. Sometimes they're not invited to a party where they'd like to be, and they almost always must cope with rejection by at least one boyfriend or girlfriend. Unfortunately, when grade-skipped adolescents encounter these typical problems, they, their parents, and their teachers tend to blame the problems on the grade skipping. If they haven't jumped a grade, however, the problems are assumed to be normal. Some research also indicates that very gifted children (those with IQs of over 145) tend to have greater social problems than more typical gifted children; thus, the assumption that grade skipping causes social problems is made by adults who are not specialized in the psychology of gifted children.

If you believe that your child is a candidate for grade skipping, find a psychologist who specializes in working with gifted children to evaluate your child. If the psychologist agrees with your conclusions after an assessment has been completed, ask the psychologist to meet with the school administration to make the recommendation for grade skipping. Sometimes the grade skip may require two steps, experimental subject acceleration occurring first. After your child has made a successful adjustment to subject acceleration, educators may be more confident of the grade skip.

20

~~~~~~

SCHOOL ABILITY
GROUPING

S chools continue to vacillate on the issues related to grouping by ability and/or achievement. *Homogeneous grouping* refers to keeping children with similar achievement levels together, whereas *heterogeneous grouping* mixes all children regardless of ability or achievement. Whichever direction the schools take, they appear to be able to cite research that supports their points of view. The reform at any one time seems to relate more to what they've done in the recent past than to what the research data clearly support. If homogeneous grouping has been used for awhile, it appears to be time for a change; on the other hand, if classes have been heterogeneously grouped, schools also perceive it must, again, be time for a change.

Parents also tend to vary in their preferences for ability grouping. However, this variation tends to be less era related and more attached to the specific group in which their own children are placed. If their children are in the highest group, parents usually prefer homogeneous grouping. If they are in middle or low groups, parents tend to prefer that schools discontinue ability groups. If they have several children who are in two or all three categories, they are very likely to have mixed feelings about grouping.

The attitudes and actions of both educators and parents are logical. For educators, neither homogeneous nor heterogeneous grouping meets the needs of all students. They tend to see only the shortcomings of the system they are using at present; therefore, change seems to signal improvement. We might call this the "grass is always greener" theory. Parents' perceptions based on their own children are also accurate. Gifted children in high achievement groups, in which curriculum is modified, tend to accomplish two grades in one year compared with those who are heterogeneously grouped. If curricular modifications are not made, the gains are much less but, nevertheless, continue to be greater than in heterogeneous grouping.

On the other hand, children in middle and low groups are not those making great gains. Although most studies show no effect on their self-esteem, loving parents would like to rescue their children from low self-esteem. Children tend to have less academic confidence if they are not achieving as well as others, whether they are homogeneously or heterogeneously grouped, but their lesser confidence is easily blamed on the faulty grouping.

When schools choose heterogeneous or homogeneous grouping, they establish clear priorities for their students. The school that refuses to group children based on academic skills is stating that social adjustment is the first priority and academic challenge is of lesser importance. When social adjustment is prioritized, academic achievement is likely to decline for gifted students and even perhaps for all students. As we try to save some children's self-concepts, we may be, in a very global way, preventing gifted students from stretching themselves mentally during a very important stage of cognitive development. Furthermore, prioritizing social adjustment becomes translated by children to mean that peer conformity is the priority value. Recent studies have indicated that adolescent peer groups are not supportive of learning and that there is a great deal of peer pressure on students who are perceived as "brainy." Removing ability grouping undoubtedly adds to the stress these teenagers feel.

It is hard to predict the educational or emotional outcome for students who are being prevented from developing their mental ability to fit socially with their peers. We may recognize the loss only after an entire generation reaches college. Other nations that value achievement are demanding much more challenging education of their students. Their students will not slow down to wait for our country's students to catch up.

Although the style of using ability grouping in schools will undoubtedly come and go and change from school to school, parents of intellectually gifted children should keep schools aware of their concern that their children require the opportunity to learn. You may wish to pose the following question to your child's principal or teacher:

Would you like to spend a year going back to learning fractions and decimals or reading eighth-grade literature?

Their answers and your answer to such a question will be "no," yet many intellectually gifted children are in similar positions, relearning skills that they learned three or four years earlier. No one expects an average child to repeat skills after they've already demonstrated competence. Why should an intellectually gifted child be punished with such meaningless learning tasks?

21

^^^

HOME SCHOOLING
AND ENRICHMENT

A lack of academic challenge in the classroom sometimes leads parents of gifted children to question
whether their children will fare better if they are home
schooled. Those who ponder this question are usually parents who have already experienced the joys and satisfactions
of teaching their children informally. They typically feel confident in their ability to challenge and excite their children
toward learning. Furthermore, they may be aware that
biographies of the eminent in most fields indicate that many
were at least temporarily home schooled or individually
tutored by a parent, relative, or adult friend. These factors,
and frustration with their children's inappropriate education
in public schools, convince parents that home schooling provides the best alternative for their gifted children.

In some rare cases, home schooling is the best alternative. Children who are home schooled for the most part learn
skills well. After all, a one-to-one tutorial can be tailored to
the specific pace and learning style of a child. There is considerable evidence of the effectiveness of tutorial instruction
for all children.

However, there is more to education than learning a
body of material. Discussion, peer interaction, cooperation,
and competition are all parts of a stimulating learning environment. Children who are home schooled don't usually

have the opportunity to interact intellectually with other students. Although a parent can certainly stimulate and encourage thinking, there is great benefit to variation and peer perspectives.

Perhaps the most serious problems that develop related to home schooling are the pressures that frequently build between parent tutor and child. Teacher and student may become enmeshed in conflict, and not only are there frequent frustrations, but in many cases the parent decides that home schooling is not as ideal as he or she had hoped. When the child is returned to the classroom environment, the problems that initiated the home schooling have often multiplied. Readjustments to the classroom are hardly ever easy.

Despite the many negatives, there are some unusual circumstances when home schooling is ideal. Some examples include temporary home schooling during a major trip that provides unusual educational opportunities; home schooling of children with extraordinary giftedness when it includes siblings or other children; and home schooling of children who live in isolated areas of the country where travel to a school is extremely time consuming.

By and large, however, it seems logical to make every effort to coordinate home and school environments so that children do most of their learning in the classroom. Although gifted children must sometimes learn to tolerate repetitive material, many teachers are sensitive to the importance of a challenging curriculum.

When children do not find sufficient challenge in the classroom, parents may often provide partial home schooling as an adjunct to the classroom curriculum. They may, for example, design out-of-school experiences that fit well with topics being addressed in school. Thus, students may prepare enrichment projects to share with their teachers and class-mates. Sometimes arrangements may be made between parents and teachers for these children to have free time away from some classroom assignments so that they may spend school time on their special projects.

If there are a number of families who become frustrated with a lack of inappropriate education for their gifted children and some of them are interested and talented in teaching gifted children, an interest in home schooling can be expanded to the founding of a small private school. Many excellent independent schools for gifted children were initiated in exactly this manner. A small private school can provide the benefits of individualization and challenge and avoid many of the pitfalls of the home-schooled family setting. It is recommended that parents do all they can to support and improve their current school, but the parent-led private school offers distinct advantages over individual home schooling.

The combination of a positive home-school relationship and flexibility by both parents and teachers usually makes home schooling unnecessary for gifted children. Alternatives suggested in this key and throughout the book may help parents with the frustrations they meet in the attempt to provide their gifted children with challenging curricula.

22

HOMEWORK HABITS

Homework is a controversial topic in many households. Gifted children vary in their responses to school expectations of homework and study. Achieving children usually study at a desk or table in a quiet place, although some listen to music. However, underachievers exhibit a great many troublesome study habits. Many are convinced that they study best while lying on their beds with headsets on, watching TV, and reading something over once quickly. Others do homework only after they're nagged, scolded, reminded, and supervised. Even then, they protest and avoid quality work. A third group of children sit with a parent nightly, certain that they can't complete their assignments without that parent's assistance and direct supervision. Finally, there are some children who simply don't do homework or study at all. They may try to convince you that their avoidance of homework is caused by lack of challenging assignments and by boredom. Some gifted children are accurately describing a problem. Many, however, have simply discovered a way to mislead you. As parents of gifted children who may be in one of these last four groups, you may wonder how your children fell into such bad habits and why other children have better habits.

Good habits begin with an appropriate time and place for study. In determining a good time, you'll need to work around your own family schedules. However, some general rules can guide you in setting both a time and a place.

Children should be allowed time for a break immediately after school to have a snack, enjoy physical activity, or chat. Many children like to watch TV during the break time; however, television places children in a passive mode, making it difficult to move them from TV to homework. It's better to insist that television follow study and homework. Explain to your children that exercise is both relaxing and energizing and is more appropriate after a day of sitting. You may also wish to use a plug lock* for your television to emphasize its nonuse before and during homework.

Children are more motivated to do their homework if they have something to look forward to after it's completed. If possible, at least part of the study time should take place before the evening meal, leaving time after study for watching television, reading, or playing games. When study time is too late in the evening, children are often tired and tend to daydream or dawdle. Most children don't like to sleep (it's adults who do), so homework can become a "stay up late" manipulation if it takes place just before bedtime.

The amount of study time varies with children's grade and school requirements. Elementary school children might study from 15 minutes to an hour; middle school children from one to one and a half hours; and high school students from one and a half to two hours per evening. Three or more hours may be required for students in highly academic high schools. Special projects may take considerably longer at almost any grade level. If children say they have completed all of their homework before the allotted study time, suggest that they use the remainder of the scheduled time for reading over material, organizing notes, or extra reading or creative writing. When children have become independent

*For information about plug locks, check your local hardware store or call 1 (800) 475-1118.

and motivated, there no longer is reason to hold them to an exact time frame. Except for long-term projects, younger children rarely have homework on weekends, so there is no need for Saturday or Sunday study time for most children.

An appropriate study place is equally important for providing an atmosphere in which children learn efficiently. Sitting at a desk with good lighting in a quiet place away from parents and siblings helps children concentrate better and become more actively involved in the material. Some children insist that they can't study without music. If you're preparing them for academic success, it seems realistic for them to develop habits that will help them adjust to environments that will open educational doors for them. (I've never heard of SATs being given with music blaring or college professors playing music in their lecture halls.) After your children have learned to concentrate in a quiet atmosphere, they may certainly introduce quiet music gradually and experimentally, provided the sound doesn't interfere with their concentration. Research indicates that television interferes even with motivated college students' learning, so parents can feel free to deny TV accompaniment during study time.

There's another advantage to separating your children from family activity during study. Dependent children, who are likely to ask questions before they've tried to solve problems on their own, are less likely to do so if Mom or Dad is physically located at a distance. It's important for your children to take the initiative to work on their homework independently before they ask for help. You should answer questions only after your children have made a determined effort to work out the material on their own. Sometimes gifted children use questioning as a way to gain attention, not because they don't understand the material. Don't sit with your children during homework time. It's their responsibility to do their homework and yours to take an interest and monitor only when appropriate.

Showing an interest in your children's homework is always important. Reading a story they've written or checking for errors in a composition might be helpful if your children request it. Discussing ideas or quizzing your children in spelling or Spanish is a fine show of support. You can also work with children on special projects; however, it is important that you offer only your guidance, not become overly involved, or they will begin to believe that the project is your responsibility instead of theirs. Furthermore, if the special project is to be graded or entered into a contest, they may feel that your excessive help is pressure and that their grade or award is not honestly deserved.

If your gifted children are underachievers, check their homework on a regular basis to be certain that they're completing quality work; however, don't correct it as a teacher would. If they've done their homework carelessly, indicate this, and let them know that members of your family take pride in their work. If it appears that they're not comprehending a concept, take time to explain it. If you see a misspelled word or an obvious error, you can point it out.

Mothers are often assigned the task of schoolwork supervision, but mothers or fathers can help their children. For boys, it's often helpful if Dad takes the major responsibility for helping with or monitoring schoolwork, especially if the child is not performing well in school. It is important for dads to communicate clearly to their sons about how important they believe schoolwork is.

Parents should always take an enthusiastic and positive interest in their children's schoolwork and learning. It makes a great difference to them!

23

PARENT–SCHOOL COMMUNICATION

Most teachers become teachers because they want to teach children. They usually care about their students. Now, you may say that you could prove that this isn't the case with some of the teachers who have taught your children. A small percentage of teachers may feel and act "burned out," may not want to teach anymore, never really wanted to teach, or thought teaching would be something different from what they're experiencing. However, the vast majority of teachers want to guide your children toward positive learning experiences.

Parent-teacher conflicts usually emerge because some teachers and parents have different philosophies about how children should be taught. Some parents believe that their philosophies are better than those of their children's teachers. The parents may be right. On the other hand, the teachers may also be right. When there is a conflict of philosophies between teachers and parents, a united parent-teacher front may be destroyed.

If the parents' educational philosophies cause them to encourage their children to do more than the teacher expects, these philosophies probably won't cause problems because the children continue to receive a message of responsibility from their parents. However, if the parents' philosophies differ from those of the teacher in such a way as to provide an unintentional "easy way out" for the children or if the parents describe a teacher's philosophies as inappropriate, irrelevant, or boring, the children are given an excuse to avoid doing what the teacher expects. Even if the parents disagree with the teacher, they should not share their perspective with the children because there is the risk that the children will assume they can escape from school responsibility with parental support.

There are some special communication problems with regard to gifted children. Many teachers who love to teach children are not particularly sympathetic to the needs of gifted children. They may even regard the provision of more challenging assignments for gifted children as elitist and unfair to the other children in their classrooms. Furthermore, because most curricula are designed for average children, teachers may assume gifted students know much less than they actually do. Your efforts to describe your children's capabilities may be met only with the too frequent assumption that you are placing pressure on your children. Also, teachers will undoubtedly remind you that there are 28 or 150 other students for whom they are responsible. Such attitudes cause parents and teachers to feel very frustrated.

Parents search for communication methods to help them become advocates for their children. There is no foolproof way, but following are sample conversations you can have with children and teachers. Be prepared to be positive, patient, and persevering when communicating with schools.

You can try the following conversation when your child comes home complaining about the work being too easy or his teacher giving too much busywork:

Jonah: Mom, it's been an awful day. All we do is write, write, write. The teacher gives us so much busy-work. I know it all already, and I just hate school.

Mom: I guess that must feel terrible. Why do you suppose your teacher gives all that work?

Jonah: She's just mean.

Mom: Well, when I think of the teachers who gave me the most work when I was a child, I think they did it because they had very high expectations for their students. Even though I complained, too, now that I look back, I guess I really learned a lot. When you think about it, if your teacher sets high expectations, it means that there will not be gaps in your education. That will help you in the future.

Jonah: Yeah, I guess so, but I sure look forward to spring vacation.

Mom: You'll deserve that vacation if you really work your hardest. I bet your teacher will realize you're an excellent student and will provide you with some especially interesting assignments.

After having this conversation with your child, you may want to notice if his assignments are, in fact, too easy or if he would just rather be watching TV. If he is indeed unchallenged, it would be good to try the following conversation with his teacher.

Mom: I came to talk to you because I wanted to share some observations about Jonah. I know you're an excellent teacher, and as his parents, we've made it clear to him that we value your challenging learning environment. Nevertheless, he says the work is too easy and complains of boredom.

Ms. James: You know, there are many smart students in Jonah's class. We're trying to prepare our students for middle school where they're given a lot of homework. What makes you think the work is too easy?

Mom: Here are some examples of complex work Jonah's done independently because he's very interested in moving ahead in math on his own. He also says he would enjoy some more challenging science.

Ms. James: This work is actually quite advanced for a student Jonah's age. You're not pressuring him at home, are you?

Mom: No, I don't believe so. He's doing this work independently. I was only hoping he could be challenged a little more in math.

Ms. James: Thanks for telling me. I'll try to eliminate some drill work and will consider special assignments. I'll also talk to Mr. Genes, his science teacher, about some special projects.

Sometimes teachers deny that a problem exists. When this occurs, don't pursue it. The teachers probably need some time to think about your concerns, and if you press them, they'll only feel that they must prove their case. Be assured that you've communicated and the teachers have heard your comments. Now permit time and thoughtfulness to bring about change.

Suppose your child comes home with stories about negative comments her teacher has made; for example, "Your mom says you're so gifted. I think you're just lazy." Of course, your child tells you this both because she actually feels hurt and helpless and also because she's hoping you'll take her side against her teacher. First, you might ask her why she thinks the teacher called her "lazy." Her response will probably be something like, "I don't know," "I didn't do anything wrong," or "She doesn't like me." Your response, in turn, could be something like this:

I know you're not lazy, so you must be doing something out of character in school. I guess you'll just have to prove yourself by working harder, and she'll probably stop calling you lazy. Not only that, I bet she'll like you better, too.

You can remind your child about how hard she worked on an important project or chore with you to encourage her viewing herself in a more positive way. This actively compensates for her teacher's negative comments, but avoids an alliance with her against the teacher. Reframe the teacher's comments each time your child expresses a complaint because, although teachers shouldn't be name-calling in the classroom, your child's effort and behavior probably require improvement, or no teacher, not even a bad one, would call her "lazy."

Although encouraging your child's improved effort and behavior should be your first priority, if you continue to hear that a teacher is using negative name-calling, report your concern to the school's principal. Absolutely do not tell your child of your report, or he or she will view it as a battle with the teacher and won't improve. Principals cannot do anything about problems unless parents share their observations with them, nor can you expect an immediate change. However, take the responsibility of communicating respectfully.

You'll feel good if you have encouraged your child's improved behavior and communicated the problem to the appropriate supervisor. Put aside your own anger, and consider how supportive you can be to your son's or daughter's educational accomplishment. Challenge the child to show the teacher that he or she is an achiever and a nice person.

You may wonder why so much emphasis has been placed on positive school communication and advocacy for your children. Here is a case study that illustrates the reason well:

> Lisa came to the clinic because she was a gifted under-achiever. She was actually to be retained in sixth grade because she had refused to do any homework assignments all year. Her report card showed all Fs, and her achievement test scores had declined. She argued with most of her teachers and was even disrespectful toward some. She was disrespectful toward her parents as well. Lisa told her psychologist that her school life became terrible after third grade when she came to her new school and that she had been an honor roll student at her old school.

> Lisa's parents reflected a similar story. They had complained to the school board and threatened to have the principal fired because they believed nothing was being done for Lisa. As a result, Lisa felt empowered to fault the school for her problems. She took no responsibility because she could easily lay the blame on others. By sixth grade, Lisa had little confidence in her own ability to reverse her underachievement.

Studies of underachieving gifted children show opposition between parents and schools to be a fairly typical pattern. Although this is certainly not the only cause of underachievement, it's easy for children who lack confidence to find scapegoats for their problems. Because schools frequently don't provide appropriate programming for gifted children, it's also very easy for parents to become negative about education. Schools are called upon to be everything to everyone, so perhaps it's not surprising that they can't fulfill all their challenges. *Positive*, *patient*, and *persevering* remain the critical traits for parent advocacy.

24

CHALLENGE ALTERNATIVES FOR GIFTED TEENAGERS

E ntrance into middle or junior high school initiates many opportunities both in and out of school that thus far have not been available to your elementary school-age children. Subject acceleration and grade skipping, described in Keys 18 and 19, continue to be alternatives for some teenagers, but now there are many new alternatives.

Talent Search, which was begun at the Johns Hopkins University Center for Talented Youth (CTY) in 1971, is conducted in many middle schools throughout the country. Seventh graders who score high (usually above the 94th percentile) on the norm-referenced achievement tests given in their schools are invited to take college entrance exams (Scholastic Assessment Test—SAT I or the American College Testing Program). Although these tests are far more challenging than any these students have ever taken, they serve to measure the advanced thinking skills of even very gifted students and identify students who are in need of more challenging programs. CTY now conducts a Young Student's Program for grades 5 and 6 in some areas.

Talent Search not only identifies gifted students; it also provides opportunities for a variety of summer and school year accelerated and enriched classes in mathematics, science, literature, foreign languages, and creative writing that have heretofore not been available.

There has been ongoing follow-up research of Talent Search students. All of it has found that participation in actual programming has been productive and motivating for students. Improved feelings of self-worth, as well as reduced arrogance, for these students also resulted from involvement in the combination of the accelerated curriculum and highly intellectual peer stimulation. Participation in the testing has no disadvantages because it provides students with practice in taking tests that they will again be required to take before college admission.

Correspondence courses for high school and introductory college credit can be another source of challenge. They are available through most major universities and are appropriate for gifted students who may wish to graduate early or take high school courses that aren't offered in their own high schools. The college credit courses are usually accepted by students' own state university systems and may be transferable to other colleges or universities as well. The grades may not be transferable, and students should certainly check with specific colleges to determine if such credits are acceptable. Completing correspondence courses without direct teacher assistance or scheduled classes takes a fair amount of self-discipline, but many students are able to accomplish correspondence courses either because of intrinsic interest in the subject or because they see it as an important step toward accomplishing an acceleration goal.

A number of states now provide specialty and residential high schools for gifted students. Some schools, such as the Illinois Mathematics and Science Academy and the Texas Academy of Health and Science, emphasize math or science.

Other residential and specialty schools specialize in the arts or the humanities. There have always been some independent and public schools that provide an advanced curriculum for gifted students.

The costs of tuition at private schools may prohibit attendance by some gifted children. Most schools give some scholarship tuition, however, and highly gifted and achieving children may be afforded these scholarship opportunities. In general, scholarship aid is related to family income, but schools vary in their formulas for providing financial assistance. Some private schools provide specific specialties; for example, the Interlochen Music Academy in Michigan is known nationally and internationally for the unique musical preparation it provides its students.

Difficult decisions face parents who consider enrolling their children in residential schools. Many of the residential high schools are located on college campuses, and some parents hesitate about sending their children into a university environment at so young an age. The greatest worry for parents is having their adolescents leave home three or four years before they typically would. Although most students make the adjustment well, family life with teenagers can sometimes be just too much fun to miss. Of course, there are more than a few parents who might say this in a directly opposite way. For them, family life with teenagers might be better if teenagers were already away at school at least some of the time.

In many junior and senior high schools, students are offered opportunities to prove competence by testing out of courses. For students who have had enriched or accelerated summer experiences or opportunities to study in other countries, examinations can be used to provide credit without the drudgery of having to take courses in which they already have knowledge. It is important for students to review and prepare for such tests and to have guidelines about what to expect. If students don't pass the examinations, this confirms only that they may not be as knowledgeable as they assumed; it shouldn't be perceived as a failure. Most students who are prepared pass such examinations, and there is a real savings of time and boredom for them.

The College Level Examination Program* offers examinations for students in thirty subject areas. Students, regardless of age, may take these tests at reasonable cost. Many colleges accept these college credits, although some do not. Students should check with the specific colleges they're considering for entrance.

Many high schools provide another desirable option to gifted students through the Advanced Placement (AP) program, which is also sponsored by College Board (see the end of the book for the College Board office nearest you). Although students can take AP courses individually, most high schools offering this option actually have AP courses taught by teachers, much like honors courses. AP courses have expanded in number and variety and include foreign language, calculus, chemistry, music theory, computer science, biology, English literature, and composition. Most courses take a full year to complete, and examinations are given by the high schools in the spring of each year. AP credits are accepted by approximately 1,300 colleges. However, some of these colleges accept only a limited number of credits. If colleges accept credits, this can be a cost-effective way for high school students to take challenging courses within their high school environment and get a jump start on a typically lengthy higher education.

*For further information, contact the College Board, Box 1842, Princeton, NJ 08541, or phone (609) 951-1026.

Early attendance at college provides several other flexible alternatives for gifted high school students. Some high schools and colleges encourage concurrent enrollment; that is, students may take college courses at a local college while continuing high school courses. These courses are usually taken during the junior or senior year, although on occasion sophomore students with unusual talents have taken college courses. In some cases, concurrent courses encourage students to graduate from high school early and attend college full time. It permits other students to graduate with their high school class, but to enter college as advanced freshmen after graduation. Students who choose to take college courses while enrolled in high school usually receive both high school and college credit for the same course. If a student is not satisfied with the college grade, he or she may choose not to transfer it to the college record. Of course, if it is transferred to a different college, the second college typically accepts the credit without the grade. Either way, the gifted high school student searching for challenge has the opportunity for early exposure to both college curriculum and environment. Early admission to college, with or without graduation from high school, is an excellent way for some gifted students to enrich and accelerate their education.

Many high school teachers and administrators discourage early graduation and early college admission. Also, gifted high school students who might consider this approach may lose the opportunity for scholarships and honors. The early college entrant must be prepared to trade some of these opportunities for the challenge of college work. If students or their parents have doubts about early full-time college work, the strategy of first enrolling part-time while still in secondary school facilitates their decision making.

Although many parents worry about sending their children to college at ages fourteen through seventeen, actual research data show that when such children are carefully screened and have been involved in accelerated and challenging programs, most make very successful adjustments. There is no evidence that students who have entered college early have more problems than other students; however, there is considerable evidence that their eventual adjustment is as good as or better than that of gifted students who didn't enter college early. Although it is true that not all students who enter college are happily adjusted, neither are all students of typical age.

Parents must explore carefully to determine what college support will be available if their adolescents enter college early. They also should be cautious when helping their adolescents to make this difficult decision. Young people should not feel pressured by parents or teachers to enter college before they are academically and emotionally mature enough to handle the special pressures to which they'll be exposed.

25

SPECIAL COLLEGE ADJUSTMENT FOR GIFTED STUDENTS

Gifted young people have some special adjustments to make in college even if they're National Merit Scholars and valedictorians of their high school classes. The first and most difficult adjustment is to the intense competition in colleges. Some of your children may have already shown strong competitive characteristics in high school; others may not ever have seemed to be concerned about competition. The latter group may not have shown their interest because they were easily at the top in intellectual or artistic arenas.

Children exhibiting either set of characteristics may experience a humbling shock when they attend a college or university in which most students graduated in the top 10 to 15 percent of their high school classes. Extraordinarily capable students who receive their first Bs for exams or compositions may suddenly feel incapable of anything or everything. Receiving grades of Cs or Ds, even after they've studied, may cause these students suddenly to lose trust in their college capabilities. Although in some ways they continue to believe they are intelligent, in other ways they find their feelings of inadequacy to be devastating. The adjustment to no longer being at the top, or simply to feeling average, can cause gifted college students to "shut down," become depressed, and avoid classes and studying.

Underachievement related to perfectionism may strike for the first time in college for many of these gifted students. The U.S. Office of Education estimates that of the top 5 percent of this country's high school graduates, 40 percent do not graduate from college. Most of these students are intellectually gifted.

Your young adults of college age require your support. They worry about disappointing you if their college grades don't meet the levels of their high school years. Don't be quick to assume the lowered grades are caused by too much partying or inattention. You may wish to state explicitly that although you recognize that they'll do their best, you understand that college can feel intensely competitive and that most students' grades do not remain as high as they were in high school. Here are some suggestions that can help gifted college students:

- Never skip a class during your first semester, no matter how boring or irrelevant you believe it to be. You've paid for this education, so you might as well get your money's worth. The lecture or explanation you miss may become the exam question for which you don't quite remember learning the answer.
- Plan to study at least two hours for each hour of class time, even if college seems easy at first. Colleges recommend this guideline; take their advice literally. Two hours is not only for the "dumb" kids; it means *all* students. Find a study place in a library or quiet room. Dormitories are hardly ever effective study places.
- Structure your study time on a schedule or calendar at least one week ahead of time. Visualizing the time allocated for study lessens the pressure you feel.
- If you're struggling with course content, find help *before* you fail. Writing labs, tutors, study groups, and counseling abound on college campuses. No one is going to take you

KEYS TO PARENTING THE GIFTED CHILD

by your hand for help; you must initiate the search, but plenty of willing and free help is available. Even students who receive As in college courses sometimes receive tutorial help.

- Schedule exercise time at least three times weekly. Daily exercise is even better. Exercise helps you feel alert and in control and provides an excellent tension release. If you schedule exercise with a friend, you are more likely to be faithful to the routine.

- Plan for brief social time daily and a little more on the weekends. Don't overallocate your social time. There is always more to do than you plan for. Weekends shouldn't be used for social life alone. Successful college students study at least part of every weekend. Remember, alcohol, drugs, and study don't mix well.

- Find friends who are serious students. The intensity of their study will inspire you to study. Surrounding yourself with friends who are "goof-offs" causes you to feel like you're overstudying even when you've done minimal work.

- Develop and keep regular, healthy eating and sleeping habits as much as possible. Fatigue and poor nourishment only increase your feelings of being overwhelmed.

- Many students can arrange to work while at college. Although the money may be important, protect your initial tuition investment by prioritizing study time before work. Ten hours a week is enough until you adjust to the rigors of college. If possible, find a job that permits you to explore vocational options or build an experience base for your future career.

Although many students begin college with a commitment to a career, course exploration may indeed cause them to change career directions entirely. Although parents should feel comfortable about discussing career implications with their children, including insights about their own careers, their children must live with their own choices. College students benefit if they can find mentors who are potential models for careers they're considering. They may wish to volunteer to assist professors or off-campus professionals to understand potential future careers better.

Parent influence can be positive, but parent attempts at control hardly ever work anyway and may justifiably result in parent-child alienation. If you've steered them in an appropriate direction during childhood, you have less to worry about. Even if you have, however, you won't be worry free. Your children may choose careers that are impractical, unrealistic, and entirely different from those you wish. Despite your disappointment, restrain your criticism. By college age, these are their choices.

Reserve your right not to waste your money. If your children are not serious, encourage them to get their own loans. Their personal financial investments will reinforce their personal effort investments.

Education after high school may be very extensive for gifted students. They may require financial support for 8 or 10 years to achieve the high-level goals to which they aspire. Match your financial contributions to their personal commitments. They are often sacrificing many years of youthful fun to invest in careers that require heavy personal commitment.

The tensions that surround dependence-independence conflicts during these years may challenge even the most loving parents. Although formal education for these gifted students may feel like "forever," their nimble minds will be challenged and the likelihood of their contributions to society will be enhanced.

26

CAREER DIRECTION AND SELECTION

G ifted children who have very specific talents are likely to find themselves motivated to explore careers that employ these talents. However, multitalented children may or may not direct themselves to a career early. Sometimes they are interested and capable in so many areas that it is extremely difficult to choose only one. Furthermore, differential aptitude tests that help more typical students find their directions may only confirm high scores for gifted students in almost every area.

Further complications of multipotentiality take place when college professors or talent coaches identify the extraordinary skills of students. One high school student, taking college courses on a large university campus, was encouraged by both her philosophy and her computer science professors to major in their areas. Neither professor realized that she was still a high school student, but both were impressed by her superior performance.

As another example, talents in music and science often go hand in hand, and two teachers separately identifying these talents may enthusiastically encourage their students to pursue these very different fields. Students with such talents often feel they can accomplish whatever they choose and may thus become even further confused.

On the other hand, gifted students may also feel pressures that come from their continued extraordinary performance. These pressures may actually prevent them from taking career risks because they fear they may not be able to continue to achieve as successfully in the adult world. One college student who wanted to be a writer confided that since attending an excellent writers' workshop, she had discontinued all her writing. She further expressed her need to do original and unique writing and ended our conversation by indicating a wish that she was not so special or intelligent.

These examples of young adult gifted students perhaps encapsulate best the issues of multipotentiality, expectations, and pressures to choose careers in which they may make unique or special contributions. These students not only require career counseling but should be receiving help from a counselor who specializes in understanding the pressures of giftedness.

Although some parents may have the background to provide their children with career counseling, other parents may have limited experience and cannot provide this guidance. If students don't go to specialized counselors, their friends become the ones they turn to for support. Unfortunately, their friends are likely to be as unknowledgeable about careers as they are.

Whether or not your young adult child is willing to seek career counseling, working in situations in which they can observe career mentors can be helpful to them. Professors in large universities are often willing to have such students as research assistants for either laboratory or library research. Professionals in business, medicine, psychology, law, and many other fields are willing to share career histories, struggles, and joys with young people.

105

Autobiographies found in libraries and bookstores may not be as personal a source as mentors, but they include a variety of opportunities for understanding career development routes. Unfortunately, in a society in which vocational opportunities change so rapidly, students may find themselves directed toward biography-inspired careers that are already overcrowded.

Gifted students are only partially well advised to follow their passions to their career choices. This often given recommendation may ignore the multiple passions of gifted students and the paucity of positions in many career areas. Several students have shared with me that their passions for singing in choirs not only led them astray in college (too much singing left little time for study) but provided no foundation at all for the world of work. Aptitudes and intense interests should be tempered by career realities. Even when students finally believe they've found their career direction, interviews with adult practitioners are critical to confirming or deterring their choices.

A rapidly changing society should also encourage students to prepare themselves for many related opportunities. It is not unusual for adults to alter their careers several times during their lives. Students who can prepare for this flexibility expand their opportunities and choices. Furthermore, intellectually and creatively gifted adults often enjoy the challenge that comes with multiple career directions.

27

PRAISE AND POSITIVE REINFORCEMENT

Biographical accounts and research on gifted achievers remind us that, as children, they received plenty of praise and positive reinforcement from their families. Typically, they were raised in environments in which parents had positive expectations of them.

It's important to praise your children. Positive comments by parents about their children's accomplishments and good qualities help them to feel good about themselves. Praise helps to build children's self-concepts.

Although it may seem surprising, sometimes praise can also be bad. If praise is too frequent, it may cause children to become dependent upon it, or it may feel meaningless because they've heard the praise so often. If praise is too extreme, it may cause children to internalize feelings of pressure when they feel they can't live up to the expectations established by the praise. Praise communicates adult values to children, and if many different adults praise vociferously, in effect this continuous extreme praise conveys to children the values of our society.

Verbally gifted children readily attract extreme praise. They talk like little "talking machines." Their adult-sounding vocabulary and complex reasoning engage and amaze adults. Grandparents, parents, neighbors, and even strangers in the supermarket are responsive to small children who comment intellectually on skyrocketing prices, the dilemmas of politics, or the state of the ozone layer as if they had in-depth knowledge on any or all of these topics. Some parents discontinue work activities or conversations with other adults to engage in discussions with precocious three or four year olds. Because typically they are astounded by the extraordinary vocabulary, they may punctuate each of the child's statements with extreme praise. They use such words as *brilliant, genius, perfect,* and *smartest,* and such comments as, "I believe you'll cure cancer" or "become president of the United States." Furthermore, if these children are physically attractive, such words as *gorgeous* and *stunning* are also added to the praise statements. If these children also show athletic prowess, parents suggest that it foreshadows the Olympics or professional baseball.

Some parents and grandparents have shared with me their ecstatic comments about their children and grandchildren using such terms as "she's the greatest" or "he's the most special child." When I explain that praise conveys parental expectations to children, they typically smile and remind me that their little girl, boy, or grandchild really is that special.

The problem is that praise truly does convey adult expectations to children. Although they appear to thrive on this extreme praise as little children, they internalize these praise statements as goals intended to be lived up to as school-age children, adolescents, and adults. If the praise statements are extreme, they are hardly ever able to perform to these extremes. "Perfect" and "brilliant" don't live in the real world of the classroom. Although being "the greatest" and "the best" may be possible in early grades for some children, as the curriculum becomes more challenging, perfectionistic goals become less possible even for highly gifted children.

Children who have received overpraise as preschoolers feel pressured when the praise diminishes. When they enter the world of school, they attempt to do what they have always done as preschoolers. They talk a lot, or they raise their hands constantly, and when they're not called on more frequently than others, they feel attention deprived. Teachers who understand their problems may help them adjust to sharing attention; unfortunately, not all teachers do. Some of them see these children as "pests," and even peers may view these adult-sounding talkers as "weird."

Gifted children who have received too much preschool praise sometimes become school phobic and lose confidence when they enter school. Even more likely, high-energy gifted children, especially boys, who can't cope with their lost sense of specialness may develop behavior problems. Typically, they're seated next to the teacher's desk. They, their parents, and their teachers often feel at a loss and wonder why these children no longer act gifted. Parents, especially mothers, are often blamed for placing too much pressure on their children. For these children, loss of attention and lack of praise cause them to feel pressured and unhappy. However, the pressure these children feel doesn't usually come from overexpectations but from overpraise that they internalized as expectation.

As a parent, you may be able to prevent this pressure problem, at least to some extent. You can praise more moderately and more realistically. You can tell your children they're smart without calling them geniuses. You can tell them they're attractive or pretty without labeling them perfect or smashing. If you praise children for hard work, good thinking, and perseverance, they'll know that you value hard work, good thinking, and perseverance. If you praise them as intelligent, innovative, or creative, they'll know you value these qualities. If you comment on their kindness and their sensitivity, this encourages these characteristics. Praise words that are within their control to accomplish are less likely to cause them to feel pressured.

You can't necessarily eradicate the extreme praise by neighbors or grandparents, but you can help to interpret it more moderately. For example, when Grandmom calls your son the smartest boy in the world, you can explain that it's only Grandmom's way of expressing her love, and she really only means that he's a smart child, not the smartest. You can't really interpret all the overpraise your son or daughter attracts, but your occasional reinterpretation helps them internalize realistic expectations. A few statements of extreme praise certainly do no harm. It's the constant barrage of overpraise that initiates their attention addiction and impossible self-expectations.

As you build your children's confidence and competence, use enthusiastic but moderate and realistic praise. Praise intermittently, not continuously. Permit children to enjoy the intrinsic rewards of their activities without becoming dependent on your constant attention. As you convey your value system to your children, avoid burdening them with the impossible pressures of being extraordinary, a genius, or perfect. Someday they will thank you for setting realistically high, but not impossible, expectations.

28

CREATIVITY,
PRETENDING,
AND LYING

The world of make-believe expands your children's imagination and is just plain fun. Whether you and your children take on the roles of animals or storybook characters or futuristic people, you and they are exercising your imaginations. Creatively gifted children often exhibit their imaginative abilities early.

Although stories are often read to children, imaginary stories can also be told to children. These stories can be expanded and embroidered by tellers and listeners. Fairy tales and favorite books can grow new endings or develop different beginnings. Illustrations, three-dimensional projects, and shows that include staging properties can expand fictional characters and plots.

Imaginative play can be part of family time and also thrives when children play alone. Some imaginative siblings or play pairs become involved in make-believe for hours and days. A carton filled with costumes gleaned from Grandma's attic or last week's yard sale adds to the fun. Yard goods left over from sewing projects or old bedspreads and blankets are excellent for habitat hangings. Save cartons from the recycler's truck. Boxes are harder to come by these days, but they serve as effective fortresses, castles, tents, ski mountains, and spaceships. Sound dimensions for drama can come from bells, whistles, old spoons, and pots and pans. Storage space may seem a problem, but consider purchasing fewer expensive toys to leave space for those that lend themselves to more creativity.

Creative children often have imaginary playmates. Don't burst their bubble by not accepting their pretend friends. Join the game of make-believe, although even pretend can go too far:

> My four-year-old daughter is gifted, exuberant, funny, strong willed, and tough-minded. She has assumed the identity of fictional characters since she was two years old, going through Maria (*Sound of Music*), Pinocchio, Cinderella, Charlotte, and Dorothy (Oz). She usually insists on being called by the character of the month and often acts the stories out. Her current person is Carly, her best friend, who is eight. A real person is more complicated. She even insisted on being called Carly when she went back to preschool. She can be very stubborn and demanding about it, although she is basically well-adjusted.
>
> Is this going too far? Should we insist on her being called by her real name? This has me baffled! Thanks.
>
> Baffled Mom*

Yes, this four year old has gone a little too far, and in my response to this mom, I suggested that she thoroughly enjoy her daughter's imaginary play for a little time each day; however, she should also explain and set a timer for when pretend time is over at home or in preschool. At that time, only real names should be used.

It is very important that imaginative children learn to differentiate pretend from real. If they don't, the pretend

*Rimm, Sylvia. *Sylvia Rimm on Raising Kids*. Watertown, WI: Apple Publishing Co., 1992.

begins to invade their real lives. They easily extend stories, fabricate, and lie so comfortably and convincingly that it becomes difficult for parents to know when to believe them. Sometimes even the children become confused. Although this kind of dishonesty is not intentional and is not the same as adult lying, it can easily lead to serious adult problems.

If your child has already begun extending her imaginative story as if it were real, don't accuse her of lying or threaten to punish her. Instead, explain to her (you probably have already) how much you want to be able to trust her and also how you value her imagination. When she's relating a story, ask her to stop briefly and label her continued story as partly pretend if she senses herself going beyond the limits of truth. This permits both you and your child to enjoy her creativity and feel confidence in her honesty. You may even wish to give her an example of how this can be done:

Stacy, when you told me that you had three kittens, I knew you were only pretending. I enjoy your stories so much, but it will help me to enjoy them and know you're honest if you tell me you're pretending.

If you make the mistake of frequently accusing your child of lying, you can expect that she'll automatically lie to protect her first story. Of course, defensive lying can become a very bad habit and serves only to cause your child to feel bad about herself. If you can help her balance the fine line between imagination and lying, you can enhance both her creativity and her honesty. Furthermore, you'll enjoy her delightful imagination within safe limits.

29

COMPETITION
AT HOME AND IN
THE CLASSROOM

Competition surrounds children both at home and at school. Parents may find that their gifted children are especially competitive, perhaps because of all the extreme praise they attract and because they frequently function so successfully in school environments. Gifted children internalize early the sense that they should be winners. Also, if the school curriculum is unchallenging, they may further assume that the winning should come easily.

Gifted children who succeed most of the time are often shocked when the competition becomes more intense and they've rarely experienced losses. Sometimes they adjust to the new competition. Other times they give up in despair. A shocking percentage of highly successful high school students drop out of college because they were not prepared for the competition in a typical college environment. "Despair" is the exact term these students frequently use to describe the frustration they feel with failure after there have been so many past successes.

Educators found that too many children feel like "losers." As a result, there has been a move away from competition in our schools to rescue children from their feelings of failure. It is true that children who perceive themselves as failures no longer have the confidence required for risk taking and therefore may close themselves off from further effort. However, teaching children to compete in society means giving them opportunities for success and failure.

Learning to function in competitive environments is not an automatic skill. Although parents want their gifted children to strive for success, teaching these children to compete also requires helping them to experience and cope with unsuccessful experiences. Children are usually spontaneously happy when they are successful; however, sometimes they may be mean or rude to others they deem to be less competent. Furthermore, if they lose, they may feel angry or sad. Sometimes they even avoid competitive arenas unless they are almost certain they can win. The risk of failure feels too frightening to them. As they avoid the many areas they perceive as competitive, they lose opportunities to learn skills and develop self-confidence. Although children cannot be expected to try everything, habits of avoidance can seriously restrict their opportunities. Furthermore, these habits can be generalized to adulthood and narrow career and interest choices. Thus, their home and school environments should provide opportunities for them to test their skills against others who are both more and less competent than they. Contests of skills can teach gifted children how to admire and congratulate others who are winners, as well as to be sensitive to those who lose or fail in a contest.

An appropriate framework for teaching competition at home or in the classroom should be balanced. Competition should not be so intense that children feel constantly pressured. Neither should they feel like they either lose or win all the time. Babying or protecting them from loss is not helpful to them in the long run, although they may express appreciation at your willingness to save them from stress. If competitive experiences are completely avoided, children cannot learn either to win or lose graciously. Therefore, parents and schools should encourage more and diverse opportunities for competition.

Consider the 4-H model. Many areas of talent in which to compete and many levels of awards invite children to take risks and take pride in their productivity. Blue, red, white, and gold ribbons decorate the showcases of crafts and science projects and plant and animal displays to reward both individual and group enterprise. Beyond the local competition is the county fair, and beyond this, youth may be chosen to compete at the state level. Competition has served well for motivating quality production for the many years of 4-H existence and continues effectively to encourage children's learning, creativity, and productivity.

If your children tend to back away from competition or are perfectionistic, it's a good idea to start them with competition against themselves, similar to the "personal best" used in track events. Personal competition at home can include using a timer to improve their time for setting the table, washing the car, or playing a musical piece with fewer and fewer mistakes. Examples of this personal competition as applied to school learning might be to improve speed in math facts by timing and charting time each day. A star or sticker on a chart can be used to mark each improvement over past performance. An example of personal best applied to school grades can reward a grade point average at least one fraction of a point beyond all past grade point averages.

Group or team competition is the next step and is a very powerful tool for teaching motivation. Team competition at home can include games in which one parent and one or two children compete against another parent and a child. Group competition in school can include informal contests between classes for fund-raising or label collecting at the elementary level or decorating the halls for homecoming at the high school level. Team sports are the classic training ground for teaching competition. The rules of good sportsmanship are the rules for fair competition and generalize well to both the classroom and life. Some academic team competitions include Future Problem Solving, Odyssey of the Mind, debate, music ensemble contests, Math Olympiad, Junior Engineering and Technological Society, Junior Achievement, Spell Bowl, and the U.S. Academic Decathlon. Most of these team competitions involve elements of individual competition as well as cooperation and thus pave the way for children to risk competing in more personal and independent directions.

Other forms of independent competition include essay and art contests, individual music contests, drama, forensics, talent search testing, scouting events, science fairs, and invention conventions.

Competition is fundamental to individualism, creativity, excellence, and achievement, and these should be real goals for gifted children, for excellent schools, and for a strong society.

30

~~~~~~

PERFECTIONISM

Gifted children are at risk of becoming perfectionistic. You want your children to strive for excellence. Quality work is a reasonable goal, but perfectionism goes beyond excellence: it leaves no room for error. The outcome must be the best. Perfectionism provides little satisfaction and much self-criticism because the results never feel good enough to the doer. Excellence is attainable and provides a good sense of accomplishment. Perfection feels impossible and *is* impossible for the doer to attain.

The pressures of perfectionism may lead to high-achievement motivation or may just as easily lead to problems of underachievement. The pressures children feel to be perfect may originate from extreme praise that they hear from the adults in their environment. They may also come from seeing adults model perfectionistic characteristics, or they may stem from the children's own continuously successful experiences that they then feel they must live up to or exceed. These pressures are only slightly different from the motivation for excellence. This small dissimilarity prevents these children from ever feeling good enough about themselves and precludes their taking risks when they fear the results will not be perfect. They avoid and procrastinate and feel anxious when they fear they cannot be good enough. They may experience stomachaches, headaches, and depression when they make mistakes or if their performance does not meet their perfectionistic expectations.

In most ways perfectionists are all-or-nothing people. They see themselves as either perfectly successful or total failures. On the other hand, some children may be only specifically or partially perfectionistic. For example, intellectually gifted children tend to be perfectionistic about their grades and abilities; others may be perfectionistic about their clothes and their appearance; some children are perfectionistic about their athletic prowess or their musical or artistic talent; some are perfectionistic about their room organization and cleanliness; and some children (and incidentally, also some adults) are perfectionistic in two or three areas, although there are some areas that apparently don't pressure or bother them at all.

Perfectionism not only affects perfectionists but also affects those around them. In their efforts to feel very good about themselves, perfectionists may unconsciously cause others to feel less good. Siblings or friends may feel angry, although they often don't know why. Sometimes they feel depressed and inadequate because they can't ever measure up to the impossible standards of the perfectionist. For perfectionists to maintain their perfect status, they may unconsciously put others down. Giving others unsolicited advice seems to reassure perfectionists of how intelligent they are. They're so determined to be impossibly perfect that causing others to feel bad has an unconscious confirming effect on their own self-concept. So, to balance the perfectionistic child in the family, there always seems to be a "bad kid" or an underachiever.

Here are some ways that you can help your children to avoid perfectionism:

- Help your children to understand that they can feel satisfied when they feel they've done their best; not necessarily *the* best. Praise statements that are enthusiastic but more

119

moderate convey values that children can achieve; for example, "excellent" is better than "perfect," and "You're a good thinker" is better than "You're brilliant."

- Explain that children may not be learning if all of their work is perfect—that mistakes are an important part of challenge.

- Teach appropriate self-evaluation, and encourage children to learn to take criticism from adults and other students. Teach them how to criticize others sensitively and constructively.

- Read biographies that demonstrate how successful people experienced and learned from failures. Emphasize their failure and rejection experiences as well as their successes. Help children to identify with the feelings of those eminent persons as they must have felt when they experienced their rejections.

- Share your own mistakes, and model the lessons learned from mistakes. Try to laugh at your own mistakes. Humor helps.

- Teach children how bragging affects others and how to congratulate others on their successes.

- Teach children routines, habits, and organization, but help them to understand that their habits should not be so rigid that they can't be changed. Purposefully break routines so your children are not enslaved by them. For example, if they make their beds daily, insist that they skip this chore on days when you're in a hurry. If you read to them at night and it's late, insist they go to sleep without reading. Occasional breaks in routines model flexibility.

- Teach kids creative problem-solving strategies and how to brainstorm for ideas that keep their self-criticism from interfering with their productivity.

- Explain to children that there is more than one correct way to do almost everything.

- Be a model of healthy excellence. Take pride in the quality of your work, but don't hide your mistakes or be constantly self-critical. Congratulate yourself when you've done a good job by letting children know that your own accomplishments give you satisfaction.

The dilemma for parents is to balance helping children to be successful and "good kids" without also causing them to be burdened by the negative side effects of too much pressure to be the best. We want our children to grow up to work hard and take pride in their work but also to feel the satisfaction they have earned.

31

~~~~~~

GIFTED CHILDREN WITH DISABILITIES

G ifted children with disabilities frequently receive much more attention for their handicap than their giftedness both within the family and in the school setting. The definition that is used at present to identify children with disabilities comes from Public Law 94-142:

> . . . mentally retarded, hard-of-hearing, deaf, speech impaired, visually handicapped, seriously emotionally disturbed, orthopedically impaired or other health impaired children, or children with specific learning disabilities who by reason thereof require special education and related services.

Except for the category of mental retardation, gifted children are as likely to have disabilities as average children. Although schools are required to provide for all children's handicaps, experts in the field of their handicaps rarely have experience or training within the area of giftedness and may thus ignore these characteristics unless they are brought to their attention by the children's parents or other teachers.

Although the term "learning disabled gifted" may sound like an oxymoron, there are in fact children who have excellent abstract thinking abilities, superior oral communication, and outstanding problem-solving skills but who may also have disabilities in the areas of short-term memory, spatial skills, visual or auditory processing, or visual-motor integration.

Some dependent underachievers show symptoms of disabilities that disappear when they reverse their underachievement; however, these symptoms may affect their self-concept and school achievement. Figure 31.1 can help parents to discriminate between disability and dependence.

School programs for gifted children with disabilities should include the same components as other programs for gifted children who do not have disabilities. Acceleration

Figure 31.1
WAYS TO DISCRIMINATE BETWEEN DEPENDENCE AND DISABILITY*

Dependence	*Disability*
1. Child regularly asks for explanations despite differences in subject matter.	Child asks for explanations in particular subjects that are difficult.
2. Child asks for explanation of instructions regardless of style used, either auditory or visual.	Child asks for explanations of instructions only when given in one instruction style, either auditory or visual, but not both.
3. Child's questions are not specific to material but appear to be mainly to gain adult attention.	Child's questions are specific to material, and once process is explained, child works efficiently.
4. Child is disorganized or slow in assignments but becomes much more efficient when a meaningful reward is presented as motivation.	Child's disorganization or slow pace continues despite motivating rewards.
5. Child works only when an adult is nearby at school and/or at home.	Child works independently once process is clearly explained.
6. Individually administered measures of ability indicate that the child is capable of learning the material. Individual tests improve with tester encouragement and support. Group measures may not indicate good abilities or skills.	Both individual and group measures indicate lack of specific abilities or skills. Tester encouragement has no significant effect on scores.

7. Child regularly exhibits "poor me" body language (tears, helplessness, pouting, copying) when new work is presented. Teacher or other adult attention serves to ease the symptoms.

Child exhibits "poor me" body language only with instructions or assignments in specific disability areas and accepts challenges in areas of strength.

8. Parents report whining, complaining, attention getting, temper tantrums, and poor sportsmanship at home.

Although parents may find similar symptoms at home, they tend to be more sporadic than regular, particularly the whining and complaining.

9. Child's "poor me" behavior appears only with one parent, not with the other; only with some teachers, not with others. With some teachers or with the other parent, the child functions fairly well independently.

Although the child's "poor me" behaviors may appear with only one parent or with solicitous teachers, performance is not adequate even when behavior is acceptable.

10. Child learns only when given one-to-one instruction but does not learn in groups even when instructional mode is varied.

Although child may learn more quickly in a one-to-one setting, he or she also learns efficiently in a group setting provided the child's disability is taken into consideration when instructions are given.

It is critical to realize that some children who are truly disabled have also become dependent. The key to distinguishing between disability and dependence is the child's response to adult support. If the child performs only with adult support when new material is presented, he or she is too dependent whether or not there is also a disability.

---

*Source: S. Rimm, *Underachievement Syndrome: Causes and Cures.* Watertown, WI: Apple Publishing Co., 1986. Reprinted with permission.

enrichment, grouping, and special counseling geared toward their giftedness and high achievement should be added to these children's programs. Although their handicaps must be considered, emphasis should be on the children's strengths and the expression of their talents.

Attention disorders seem to be a frequently diagnosed disability in gifted children. Attention deficit-hyperactivity disorder (ADHD) and attention deficit disorder (ADD) are characterized by high energy and difficulty with concentration, distractibility, impulsivity, disorganization, and hyperactivity for the first diagnosis and all characteristics but the last for the second diagnosis.

The DSM-III-R* considers a child to have an attention disorder if he or she exhibits at least eight of the following characteristics:

1. Often fidgets with hands or feet or squirms in seat
2. Has difficulty remaining seated when required to do so
3. Is easily distracted by extraneous stimuli
4. Has difficulty awaiting turn in group situations
5. Often blurts out answers to questions
6. Has difficulty following through on instructions from others, for example, fails to finish chores
7. Has difficulty sustaining attention in tasks
8. Often shifts from one uncompleted activity to another
9. Has difficulty playing quietly
10. Often talks excessively
11. Often interrupts or intrudes on others
12. Often does not seem to listen to what is being said to him or her
13. Often loses things necessary for tasks or activities at school or at home
14. Often engages in physically dangerous activities without considering possible consequences

*Excerpted from *Diagnostic and Statistical Manual of Mental Disorders*, Third Edition, Washington, DC: American Psychiatric Association, 1980.

Unfortunately, a fair number of these characteristics are found in many high-energy, high-intensity gifted children. If the school curriculum is not sufficiently challenging, distraction, working on two activities simultaneously (for example, reading a book while the teacher is teaching math), misbehaving, or daydreaming becomes characteristic of these children's traditional escapes from boredom.

Because ADHD is considered a disorder, the characteristic symptoms are assumed by many to signal a biochemical problem that should be treated by medication (for the most part, Ritalin). The diagnosis frequently removes the responsibility or guilt from parents and teachers who are, as a matter of fact, struggling with a strong-willed, high-energy, or difficult child.

It is always tempting to latch on to a "sure cure." However, it is critical that parents and teachers know that *all* tests for attention disorders are observational and that there are absolutely *no* definitive biological tests for attention deficit disorders at this time.

Ritalin, the main medication for ADHD, is sometimes overused and misused. One teacher of gifted children reported that half of her students were taking Ritalin for ADHD. Another gifted child who was taking Ritalin exhibited multiple side effects, including tremors and tics. Although Ritalin may calm a great many children, even help them focus attention, it is important to know that Ritalin has established side effects for many children, including loss of appetite, tics, insomnia, nausea, stomachaches, headaches, depression, social withdrawal, and loss of energy.

If most of the symptoms of attention disorders can be controlled behaviorally, medication can be avoided for many of these children. A few children require both medication and behavioral help.

Behavioral changes include learning to set clear limits for your children, although this may not be easy. Following through without overreacting is helpful. Consistency between you and your spouse is critically important. Attention to the positive is also important. There are also techniques for teaching children to help themselves to concentrate and avoid behavior problems. Specific classroom approaches to foster in-seat behavior and withdrawal of negative attention are effective. Negative attention given to children who are perceived as "bad kids" serves only to perpetuate their negative behaviors.

Before you decide that medication is the answer to your child's behavior and concentration problems at home and school, ask yourself these questions:

1. Do you and your child's other parent(s) disagree on how to discipline your child?
2. Do you frequently find yourself being negative and angry with your child?
3. Do you lose your temper often and then apologize and hug your child afterward?
4. Do you find yourself in continuous power struggles with your child, after which you feel quite helpless?
5. Do you find yourself sitting with your child to help with schoolwork because it wasn't finished in school and your child can't concentrate at home?
6. Do you find yourself disorganized and out of control much of the time?
7. Does your child spend two hours or more a day in front of a television or computer?
8. Is your workload so overwhelming that you have little time for quality parent-child time?
9. Does your child concentrate well in areas of special interest or high motivation?

10. Does your child have a sufficiently challenging curriculum in school?
11. Is your child involved in appropriate out-of-school activities for energy release?
12. Does your child know how to function well in competition?

If your answer is yes to most of the first nine questions and no to the last three, your child's symptoms of attention disorder can likely be improved by home and school adjustments. More effective parenting will help you and your child and, unlike medication, causes no negative side effects. Parenting has never been easy, but it is probably more difficult in our society today than ever before. As always, helping parents and schools work with this challenging generation of children may make a great difference and help us to avoid automatically medicating high-energy, intense children. Some children require medication to improve their concentration, but the National Association of School Psychologists recommends that medication be considered only after appropriate home and school interventions are attempted for a reasonable period of time.

All children have learning style differences that should be considered in planning their school and home learning programs. Intellectually and creatively gifted children may exhibit these differences more intensely. Parents and teachers who encourage their gifted disabled children's strengths while providing them with techniques to overcome their problems can guide these children with extreme differences toward self-confidence and achievement.

32

~~~~~~

TALENT IN THE ARTS

Artistic talent typically shows itself early; however, a three year old's outstanding violin performance or a toddler's unusual scribbles are not necessarily predictive of an Isaac Stern or a Pablo Picasso. According to retrospective studies of artists, the seeds of talent were readily observable early, although parents or teachers rarely predicted with certainty that preschooler artistic production would result in extraordinary adult performance or creation.

Biographies that describe the early childhoods of artists and musicians indicate that there was always a home environment hospitable to the emerging talent of the child. Parents themselves were frequently their children's first teachers and were often creators or performers themselves. Siblings were generally involved in the art form also, although sometimes they exhibited somewhat less talent.

Outside the family, first teachers were typically positive and supportive of the child's artistic talent, rather than disciplinarians or highly critical. As talents emerged, later teachers set high expectations, inspired their students to excellence, and led them to competitive opportunities in their talent areas. Once it was clear to the family that a child had unusual talent, adult attention was usually centered on providing the child with appropriate talent-enhancing opportunities, sometimes at the sacrifice of time spent with other family members. For the extraordinarily talented child, there was a sense of specialness as well as a drive for intense work in the child's area of talent.

For parents of children gifted in the arts, there are some guidelines found within the biographies of artists. Whether your children's special art form is music, dance, painting, or some other artistic arena, they first require the opportunity to express themselves. If intrinsic interest shows itself, it can be enhanced by your encouragement, support, and unpressured instruction. As your children's talents emerge, increasingly high-level teachers can objectively advise you and your children to understand the extent of their talents. It may be difficult for parents to be objective and critical as the children become further advanced in their specialty areas. However, continuing with only one teacher during the learning years can provide a biased view of your children's talents. Also, as you find yourself making sacrifices of both finances and time, monitor carefully the matching investment of time by your children and the credibility of their talents compared with those of peers at contests, exhibits, or concerts.

Although biographies of those who are successful in the arts tell us of artistic numerators, they do not describe the denominators. Many who were talented in the arts as children and whose parents fostered their talents by both encouragement and personal sacrifice were not successful in the arts as adults. Many, as adults, play the piano at restaurants as a second job, teach small children to play the violin, or exhibit their paintings at small art fairs while doing more mundane work to feed their families. The term "starving artist" is not without foundation. Although all involvement in the arts, avocational or teaching others, can be perceived as worthwhile, it is often a disappointing conclusion to a childhood of devotion and sacrifice. Furthermore, there are gifted flutists who have laid down their flutes never to return to them except with thoughts of depression and anger, gifted dancers who cannot even tolerate visiting a dance recital, and easels and brushes that decay and cameras that rust from disuse and disappointment.

Although most parents value artistic talent in their children, they usually recognize that only limited career opportunities exist even for those with extraordinary talents. Therefore, while parents enrich, enhance, sacrifice, and dedicate themselves to their children's special talents, they must also encourage reality testing and help children to develop fallback interests and career skills. Most of all, their children should not feel the pressured expectations that cause them to feel like failures if they are unable to attain the extraordinarily high levels of performance and competition demanded of the arts in our society. If children are prepared psychologically for the risks as well as the expectations, they are better able to adjust to moving from such goals as soloists or lead actors to membership in choral groups, orchestras, or community theaters. They are able to accept less prestigious opportunities, and if finally, even after all their efforts, they do not qualify as sufficiently talented, they can turn elsewhere for their livelihoods and continue in their talent areas to enrich their lives for their own personal or family satisfaction. They will continue, it is hoped, to appreciate the performances of others with a special depth enhanced by their own investments in their talents.

The paradox of great artistic talent is that it is an extraordinary gift and is very sparsely distributed in any population. Although a lifetime of dedication and commitment is required to cultivate this unusual gift, there are few opportunities for extraordinary artists to achieve great success. Even with the combined talent and commitment, there is no way to predict with certainty that your musically or artistically talented child will be able to attain the heights parents have the right to expect. Perhaps the artist's journey can be compared to scaling Mount Everest—the risk is great, the climb is arduous, and the precipices precarious. Even when the peaks are within view, climbers may not be able to attain them. The climb down is frightening but faster and may even involve life-threatening falls. From the foot of the mountain, the peaks remain visible. When artists have attempted to climb their personal Mount Everests, living in the shadows of the mountain may feel forever frustrating and unfulfilling. However, civilization has benefited immensely from the many artists who have risked the climb to make both small and large contributions. Young people committed to the arts deserve support from parents, teachers, and mentors.

33

~~~

RISK TAKING FOR INHIBITED GIFTED CHILDREN

A lthough it is probably true that some children are inhibited from birth, all children can learn appropriate increased risk taking. Your first step as parents is to remove the word *shy* from all conversations with or about your children. The word often becomes a negative and limiting label for children, and whether you address them directly or talk about them to other adults within their hearing (referential speaking), the label limits their sense of personal control. The more frequently children are referred to as shy, the less they feel they can control the shyness. Instead, assume that your children will participate in activities and stay positive about their participation.

When you notice shy children making an effort to be more social, praise them in a quiet, matter-of-fact way. If you exaggerate your praise, this may cause them to feel pressured about their shyness. You may also want to mention the increased maturity to other adults, preferably within the child's hearing. Here is an amusing case study:

> Mr. and Mrs. Brandt had come to the psychologist to talk about their son, Karl, who was highly anxious. They also asked for some advice relative to their daughter, Christina, who, at age three, was extremely shy. The ther-

apist suggested that they consider whether they were commenting on Christina's shyness referentially (within her hearing). They acknowledged that they were, and the therapist explained how to use referential speaking positively. The conversation was then redirected to Karl.

Three years later, Mr. and Mrs. Brandt returned to visit the psychologist. This time it was in regard to Christina. They reminded the psychologist about the suggested change in referential speaking. They also explained that it had been so effective, that they now needed help with Christina's too aggressive behavior. Wistfully, they longed for a small amount of her earlier shyness to show itself again.

Not all shy children become quite as courageous as Christina, but it is helpful for parents to teach shy children some risk-taking behaviors.

Shy children often need to be supported, encouraged, and, yes, even forced to become involved in some activities. However, select the important activities, and then be matter-of-fact and firm. You may even permit your children to choose any of two or three activities, but insist on their making a choice. Avoid power struggles. Don't get into a pattern of telling your children that they should become involved and then permit them to persuade you to change your decision.

Insist that your children participate in at least one group lesson or interest for health, safety, and physical fitness; for example, swim lessons, dance, gymnastics, baseball, soccer, tennis, and basketball offer various alternatives from which they may choose. Give them a time limit for making the choice, and then sign them up for the activities they've chosen. Drop them off at the activities, and leave. Don't stay to witness their agony, and they will make less fuss. Ignore any tears; they'll recover. The activities will become routine and will help your children to build confidence. Soon they'll be signing themselves up for more activities.

Play competitive games at home, and be sure you don't always let your children win. If they withdraw or pout, ignore the pouts, and go on having family fun. If they rejoin the game, count them in, but don't give any special notice to their joining you. If other family members tease them about being a poor sport, don't protect them. They'll soon learn to protect themselves by overcoming their problem.

Finally, try to get your children involved in group competition. Some examples of group competition are Future Problem Solving, Odyssey of the Mind, music ensemble contests, and sports teams.

As your children mature and progress, they also develop the confidence to become involved in individual competitions such as essay and art contests, individual music competitions, forensics, science fairs, and invention conventions.

If your children complain about loneliness problems in school, brainstorm a few alternative solutions to the problem together. Suggest that they practice role-playing conversations with you for solving the problem. Pretend you're the teacher or their friends, and practice giving your children possible positive and negative responses so they won't be too devastated if the teacher or children don't respond as they'd like. They need to learn to risk accepting no and realizing that they can't always please adults or peers but, nevertheless, can continue to be assertive.

Be empathic if your children are feeling lonely, but explain that most other children also experience some loneliness. You may even wish to reframe their loneliness as experience for independence. Explain that learning to be independent, and even different, can be very difficult; however, it is a life skill that will help them forever. There are likely to be many negative peer experiences to which they'll be exposed, and they require courage and independent strength to face them. Practicing independence early is good preparation for the teenage years ahead.

The most intense period of peer pressure for children is during the junior high or middle school years, and your children may feel that they must stay away from other children who may be pressing them to accept values with which your children are not comfortable. Although you should certainly encourage them to invite friends to visit occasionally, please be careful that the invitation is not mandatory. Parents' anxiety about their children's lack of friends may actually cause children to feel more anxious and may even prevent them from acknowledging that they feel lonely.

When shy children attend middle school, they should be encouraged to participate in extracurricular activities at school. Drama, forensics, debate, and the school newspaper are good for encouraging your children's assertiveness and confidence. Encourage your children's interests and participation with groups of children who share their interests. Shy children gain courage when they have interests they love to talk about. Stamp collecting, sports cards collections, drama, art, music, science, computers, hiking, and camping are all areas of interest that can encourage their excitement and shared experiences with other children. Interest-centered summer camps can provide them with friendship opportunities that may continue long after camp is over. Attendance at interest-centered conferences will introduce them to friends of all ages. Letters, telephone calls, and visits keep in-depth, interest-centered friendships alive for many years and prevent the loneliness that shy children may feel.

Closer family relationships often result when friends are not around to distract from family activities. Let your children know that they can always count on family interests, fun, and support, and their loneliness will be minimized. As your children grow older, they'll find more friends with common interests, and they'll feel appreciative that you didn't pity them just because other children didn't accept them. It is better that children grow in independence rather than become peer dependent. Although the ideal is somewhere in between, don't minimize the strengthening experiences your children are having.

Your shy children need to take small steps forward, so please view these suggestions as a long-range plan with noncompetitive activity involvement initially. As they progress in confidence, introduce one new opportunity at a time. Most important, be positive. Focus your attention on small steps forward, and try to ignore the regressions.

For some very gifted children, differences between them and their age mates are so extreme that finding peers is almost impossible. The good news is that beyond high school, social opportunities improve considerably, and your children's intelligence will no longer be viewed as a disadvantage. Instead of increasing their inhibition, your children's intelligence will increase their confidence and reduce their inhibition.

34

CREATIVE THINKING

reative thinking is a type of giftedness that may be subject or talent specific or may be generalized to all of life. Creative thinkers conclude beyond the obvious, originate or organize unique ideas, and are imaginative. They are more likely to thrive in homes and classrooms in which unusual ideas are valued and encouraged and to lose confidence in environments that are rigid or intolerant of differences.

As small children, creative thinkers may feel confused in classrooms that emphasize speed and correct answers. Their answers may not be immediate or definite. They tend to think in "multicolors" rather than "black and white." Thus, their answers to simple questions are typically more complex, elaborate, or ambiguous. This may cause them problems in classroom assignments that are directed to one answer, or even in standardized testing in which they may overinterpret or misinterpret questions and lose time in the analytical process.

Although some children seem to be born with creative insights, all children can be taught to be more creative thinkers. Creative attitudes and creative thinking techniques should be taught both at home and in the classroom. They enhance children's abilities in whichever interest direction they choose.

Cultivating creative characteristics and attitudes in your children encourages their creative thinking. Research indicates that the characteristics of highly creative children include confidence, independence, enthusiasm, curiosity, playfulness, humor, esthetic interests and involvement, appropriate risk taking, and a generally high number and level of interests. Creative persons typically feel comfortable in their aloneness and tend to have a few good friends rather than many friends. Their friends are often of varying ages and interests. Creative persons tolerate ambiguity well and may even enjoy it. Here are a few examples of how you can cultivate these creative characteristics:

• Encourage your children to spend some time alone. If they are continuously surrounded by friends, they cannot learn to enjoy being alone, nor will they have the time to develop creative interests.
• Your children may make friends who are older or younger and who have different interests. Accept their unusual friendships (within reasonable value guidelines).
• Pursue your own creative interests, and share them with your children. You will be a creative model.
• Value your children's creative ideas and products, and encourage their creative attitudes.
• Don't worry if you have to move several times while your children are young. Many creative adults have moved often during their childhoods.

Creative thinking techniques can also be taught. Some examples of techniques to teach children include analogic thinking, brainstorming (see Figure 34.1), attribute listing, morphological synthesis, idea checklists, synectics methods, fantasy analogy, implementation charting, and visualization. There are many more. Figure 34.2 is an example of how you can help your children use creative problem solving to cope with a peer problem.

Books listed at the end of this book (Additional Reading) can lead you to many approaches for teaching the creative process. Many books have been written on the topic

Figure 34.1
GROUND RULES FOR BRAINSTORMING*

---

1. **Criticism is ruled out.** This allows deferred judgment, which contributes to the creative atmosphere so essential to uninhibited imagination.

2. **Freewheeling is welcome:** the wilder the idea the better. Ideas that seem preposterous sometimes lead to imaginative yet workable solutions.

3. **Quantity is wanted.** This principle reflects the purpose of the session: to produce a long list of ideas, thus increasing the likelihood of finding good problem solutions.

4. **Combination and improvement are sought.** This lengthens the idea list. During the session, students spontaneously "hitch-hike" on each other's ideas, with one idea inspiring the next.

Source: Adapted from Alex F. Osborn (1993). *Applied Imagination*. Reprinted with permission from the publisher and copyright holder, CEF Press, Buffalo, NY.

of creative thinking, and you will also find much information in your library or bookstore to guide you.

As you encourage your children's creativity, bear in mind that even creativity can become too extreme. Key 35 explains how creativity can go awry and can cause gifted children underachievement problems in the name of creativity.

Figure 34.2
CREATIVE PROBLEM SOLVING TO HELP YOU WITH FRIENDS*

Sometimes you may find yourself being teased or hurt by others. Here's a way to solve this problem.

1. First, ask yourself what the problem is. Tell yourself what is happening that you find objectionable.

2. Then, think about all your options. Consider all the possible responses you might give to the problem. Brainstorm for ideas, observe other kids' responses, and ask adults for suggested options.

3. Choose the best option, and try it out.

4. Evaluate the success of your trial. Did it work?

5. Determine how you might improve it under new circumstances or whether you should try a different option.

6. Remember that you are usually better off confronting a person or dealing with a problem in privacy. If you try to respond in front of other kids, the other person will feel embarrassed; this hardly ever works.

Source: Rimm, S. B., *Student Stepping Stones*, Watertown, WI: Apple Publishing Co., 1990. Reprinted with permission.

35

‸‸

CREATIVE UNDERACHIEVERS

U nderachieving children are not always creative, and creative children are not always underachievers. However, there seems to be an alarming number of highly creative capable children who are not achieving well in typical classrooms. Parents of these highly creative children frequently conclude with a certain amount of pride that their children have always "marched to the beat of a different drummer."

Some highly creative children have reputations for causing some problems in school. You may wonder if schools are providing appropriately creative programs or whether you, as parents, are causing the problem. These questions may continue to plague you as you see talented but unhappy children. Here's an example:

> Bob, a sixth grader, hated school and hated his teacher. He protested on a daily basis about being bored. He loved to read and often read a book beneath his desk when he was supposed to be doing math. Although he was bright, fluent, and verbal, he rarely completed assignments. Despite his dislike of school written work, he took pride in a collection of adventure stories that he had written but wouldn't share with the teacher. He was frequently disciplined by the teacher and had earned a reputation for being the "bad kid" of the class. His parents were engaged in a continuous battle with the school, and his father maintained that schools had not

been creative enough for him, either. Dad admitted somewhat proudly, that he, like his son, had also "marched to the beat of a different drummer."

Highly creative underachievers have some similar characteristics. IQ scores tend to be in the above average to superior ranges (mostly in the 120s) rather than in the very superior range. Creativity test scores are usually above the 75th percentile and by adolescence typically exceed the 90th percentile. The characteristics and interests of these children appear to become more dramatically nonconforming and creative with maturity. IQ scores and creativity scores vary conversely as age increases. IQ scores tend to decrease as creativity scores increase.

Creative underachievers tend to have dominant rather than dependent personalities (see Key 40); that is, they insist on being in control of home, school, and peer activities. If things are not done their way, they may withdraw completely from participation. They seem determined to attract attention to their uniqueness. They usually admit that they enjoy being different, although some will describe loneliness because of their differences.

Creative underachievers, as well as creative achievers, are given a message early about the importance of creativity by at least one parent. This comes most simply by the praise given to children for their creative products and actions. They learn that when they do something unusual, or if they have a funny or different idea, this brings attention. If it is internalized as a personal and positive motivation to be creative, it does not necessarily lead to underachievement. An early indicator of a potential problem is in the differential valuing of the child's creativity by two parents; for example, Mother values creativity and Father doesn't, or vice versa. The child who identifies with the creative parent is likely to be creative, but if the other parent does not value that creativity, the seeds of opposition and underachievement are already planted.

At the elementary school level, these children may be seen as achievers, although the telltale signs of creative opposition are usually already visible. They may already be voicing complaints about "boring" reading workbooks and "teachers who don't like them." Parents may ally with them against a teacher, justifying their requests for less busywork and more opportunity for individual expression. They may also side with these children on such issues as extending time deadlines for assignments to permit their creative production or convincing principals that too strict discipline is unfair. Conversations by parents with other adults that take place within children's hearing include references to the lack of creativity in schools or the inadequacy of specific teachers.

The elementary age child develops early the power that comes with an alliance of control with one adult against a system. The school curriculum is interpreted by these children and a one-parent ally as inadequate in terms of interest and creativity. The alliance does not necessarily result in educational harm to the child. It may be productive if the adult and child are realistic in assessing the problem, the curriculum is adjusted, and the child is then expected to conform to these modifications. If the assessment of the problem is not appropriate, or even if it is appropriate and parent and child do not effectively change their attitudes, the child may respond by not conforming to the requirements of the teacher and feels justified in this opposition. The child then gains too much power in the alliance with a parent against the teacher. The creative underachiever begins a pattern of oppositional nonconformity.

Oppositional young people are faced with impossible pressures. Their internalized value system says to be creative. They translate this to mean *don't conform.* By early adolescence, parents are concerned about their children's underachievement and are trying to communicate the importance of achievement. To the child, this message is interpreted as a message to conform. Peers are also demanding conformity for acceptance. Conforming to peers also seems antithetical to these youths' wish to be creative. During these preadolescent years, creative underachievers are typically at their least happy selves, sometimes feeling unappreciated by parents, teachers, and peers alike.

By senior high school, opposition is firmly entrenched as a lifestyle. The opposition that began as an alliance with one parent against a teacher has expanded to become opposition against the other parent or both parents and any number of teachers. The manipulated ally varies. The most likely alliance group of all, however, is an oppositional and "different" peer group. Our creative underachievers have finally found acceptance by friends who also value nonconformity. They join an alliance with an openly oppositional peer group, determined to be as different as possible from what parents and teachers expect.

There is a fine line of balance between conformity and creativity. When creative children feel so internally pressured to be creative that they define their personal creativity only as what they are against, they risk losing the opportunity to develop their unique talents. If you as parents and their teachers can foster their creative productivity and can avoid facilitating escape or avoidance of responsibility in the name of creativity, these creative children can channel their important talent toward productive contributions. Here are some suggestions for parents:

145

1. A parent should not, if at all possible, ally with a child against another parent or a teacher in the name of creativity.
2. Encourage creative children to be productive in at least one area of creative expression at all times, and help them to find an audience for their performance.
3. Find appropriate achieving role models or mentors in areas of children's creativity.
4. Find a peer environment that combines creativity and achievement so that these children may feel comfortably accepted by other achieving and creative young people.
5. Encourage intrinsic motivation while also encouraging children to participate in competitive contests.
6. Use creative strengths to build weaknesses.
7. Encourage self-discipline within creative endeavors.
8. Help creative adolescents to plan creative futures.

36

GENDER ISSUES FOR GIRLS

Your gifted daughters are growing up in a generation of increased opportunities. Professional doors have opened for females in almost all fields, although data continue to acknowledge that a "glass ceiling" effect interferes with women's upward mobility in high-level positions. Some people proclaim that changes in opportunities for gifted women have not evolved rapidly enough; however, most who have experienced them are ecstatic at the choices now available to females. Despite the distance to go before society arrives at true equality, your daughters must be prepared for a different society from the one you learned about from your childhood Barbie Doll play days.

Some main issues emerge in parenting gifted daughters. Assertiveness and independence are primary. The encouragement of mathematics and science interests is also critical. There remains too much emphasis on appearance in relation to attractiveness to males. Professional female role models continue to be lacking in some areas, although surely there are more than ever before. The challenge of combining motherhood with career success probably creates the greatest stress for females.

Parents may disagree on whether their gifted daughters should direct their lives primarily toward careers, but hardly any argue about providing educational opportunities to young women that would enable such choices. Research documents that women who take the roles of full-time home-makers tend to have lower self-esteem than those who choose total career lifestyles or those who combine both. If women are going to prepare for careers, they must learn the personality characteristics required for success in a dual-gender career world.

Characteristics that are stereotyped as "masculine" are, interestingly, also typical of successful people, for example aggressiveness, ambitiousness, analytical ability, assertiveness, competitiveness, leadership ability, independence, and self-reliance. Stereotypical "feminine" characteristics include those that might be associated with mothering or, at best, a narrow range of nurturant, female-dominated occupations, for example affection, cheerfulness, compassion, gentleness, love of children, shyness, understanding, and warmth. Furthermore, books, television, and films for the most part continue to promote those gender-role stereotypes as preferable. Thus, if women are to be groomed for successful careers, parents and teachers need to praise and promote assertiveness. Fathers, especially, will need to encourage their daughters to speak their opinions. Furthermore, they need to admire overtly the assertiveness of their daughters, or girls will consider it unfeminine to be assertive.

The marriage model of how husbands and wives can share assertiveness and power continues to be precarious in real life. Because parents often continue to struggle with power issues, it is important for them to discuss how teaching assertiveness and independence is likely to shape their daughters' futures. Girls need to be inspired to be more courageous, to take risks, and to build confidence. Some suggested books to encourage girls' assertiveness by providing success models from literature are listed at the end of the book.

Mathematics ability differences between the genders breed much controversy. The nature-nurture question is continuously debated. Are females born with less potential for mathematics than males, or does our culture cultivate math anxiety and lesser skills in females? Even if genetic differences have some effects, environment can make a great difference.

Girls' interest in math can be encouraged initially by their parents. If mothers hated math, they need not advertise their distaste to their daughters. Spatial and number games and toys, including cards, checkers, chess, computer games, puzzles, board games, Legos, and construction toys, should be part of the play collections for both girls and boys. Toys that encourage spatial experiences may contribute to mathematics aptitude. Math problem solving, whether it relates to planning a new room, shopping, or football yard gains, enhances children's early mathematics comfort. Because mathematics is a threshold skill for many high-status positions, girls who are not confident or competent in mathematics narrow their career choices considerably. Even if they don't choose a career with mathematics emphasis, the society they live in requires a mathematical baseline of skills for almost everything, from completing one's income tax to becoming active in financial investments.

Emphasis on beauty and thinness needs to be redirected for girls if, indeed, they are going to view themselves as individuals rather than become dependent upon their fathers' or boyfriends' admiration. Giving young women the message that they are more than their bodies alone is difficult. Societal emphasis on beauty causes parents to pass the message "beautiful is better" on to their children. Research suggests that attractive girls and women have some advantages in their development from gifted and pretty adolescents to

149

good-looking executives. However, the extreme emphasis on excruciatingly thin models, high fashion, and continuous shopping that distracts girls from being thinkers and doers leads them to hide their intellectual, artistic, or creative gifts behind a facade of empty femininity. It makes good health sense to teach good nutrition, regular exercise, cleanliness, and *reasonable* attractiveness, considering that approximately 10 percent of college women today struggle with serious eating disorders, such as bulimia and anorexia. Their wish to be perfectly thin often interferes dramatically with their potentially productive functioning in school and in careers. Both fathers and mothers have responsibilities for giving these clear messages about appearance to their children without the exaggerated emphasis promulgated by advertising.

Finally, mothers who may have temporarily chosen the "mommy track" or are struggling with the "supermom" goal of combining parenthood and careers can be wonderful role models for their daughters. It is important, however, that these mothers communicate to their daughters the satisfaction and value of their careers. Women didn't choose to join the work force only because they wanted to earn salaries but because a career is potentially more fulfilling than working only in the home.

Your daughters need to know that work helps you to feel good about yourselves and permits you to make contributions to society. As mothers, you need to tell your daughters that you take pride in doing quality work and in fully earning your salaries. Explain that although you may be tired at the end of each workday, your weariness comes with the satisfaction of accomplishment.

Don't apologize to your children for your careers. Instead, emphasize what good role models you are and what important work you do. Both your daughters and sons will take a new pride in your accomplishments and their own. However, supermoms must also put aside their work and find time for fun and laughter.

Most mothers miss their children when they're working. They feel some guilt at not being with their children. However, by modeling independence and responsibility, working mothers are fostering their children's independence and responsibility. Children respect their mothers more because they value themselves. Daughters (and sons) also gain confidence by taking responsibility for doing more for themselves rather than depending on Mom to do for them.

Most women, and some men, too, struggle with the guilt of playing so many roles. Their guilt may not go away, but they get better at managing it if they stop apologizing for it and pat themselves on the back instead.

Career women and those who can combine parenting with their careers can be good role models for their children's female friends as well. Furthermore, as parents you may be able to introduce your daughters to women friends, colleagues, or leaders in their own fields who can help you to inspire your daughters to challenge themselves. Gifted girls have often found a lack of woman role models, particularly in the many male-dominated professions.

Women wanted the opportunity to work outside the home. Combining careers with family responsibilities is not easy for women, but they will walk with their heads higher, and so will their daughters. Women should value what they accomplish, and their daughters will, too.

37

~~~~~~

GENDER ISSUES
FOR BOYS

The world has changed for gifted boys, but not nearly as drastically as for girls. The showing of emotions, the sharing of feelings, and, most of all, nurturant parenting are now much more acceptable for young men. In the past, men often felt pressured to hide these aspects of their personalities.

Parents often express ambiguous feelings about sons who wish to play with feminine toys or costumes. A son's lack of interest in sports or a preference for the arts often frightens parents and reflects a societal homophobia. Single female parents frequently feel inadequate because they may find it difficult to provide male role models for their sons, and gifted men struggle to identify how they can be nurturant parents and also model masculinity and success.

Parents mostly require reassurance about the issue of *homophobia*, the fear of homosexuality. Although there is evidence that homosexual men sometimes played with stereotypical girl toys as children, there is also plenty of evidence that, as children, heterosexual males also played with dolls, makeup, costumes, jewelry, dishes, and so on. An interest in playing house or make-believe is normal for both males and females. Actually, mothers rarely view such play as problematical, but fathers sometimes voice anxious concerns when they see their sons engaged in such play.

Some parents become overly concerned about their sons' lack of interest in sports. When boys or girls are not involved in sports, there may be many reasons for their lack of involvement. Sometimes their disinterest is related to poor coordination or fear of functioning in competition. It can also be related to their interest in so many other areas that there is simply not enough time remaining in their hectic schedules for involvement in sports. Boys' nonparticipation in sports is also often directly related to the lack of interest displayed by their parents. It is certainly inappropriate to define masculinity in terms of sports interest and aptitudes. On the other hand, nonparticipation in sports should not serve as psychological protection for your sons from their involvement in competitive activities or physical fitness. Gifted children often have so many successful experiences in academics or arts that they fear taking risks in areas in which they may not be as successful. If you believe your sons are avoiding competition, involvement in less competitive team sports may help them learn to function better in competition. For example, the swim team or soccer seems to teach teamwork and competition without placing too much pressure on individuals. Physical fitness activities, such as hiking, biking, swimming, and track, encourage children to develop healthy bodies and strong self-concepts. Backyard sports and intramural team activities, such as volleyball, basketball, or baseball, are also facilitative to improving coordination, health, and sportsmanship.

Although there is little advantage in being involved in sports for typical nonathletic young men, there is great advantage in building physical fitness and great social advantage in learning the language of sports. Listening to conversations between boys and men will convince anyone that some knowledge of sports eases communication barriers. Talking about who won the baseball game is much like talking about

153

the weather; it's what you say after you say hello. Traditionally this is male conversation, but word has it that females, too, have increased their interest in sports; thus, a little knowledge from the sports news may ease introductory communication for both genders.

Boys should not be deprived of opportunities to share feelings and express emotions. Some boys do this quite naturally, others are afraid to, and still others would simply rather not. Parents can encourage their sons to express emotions without nagging them. If parents can express their own feelings to their sons and allow them time to respond, modeling and encouragement occur. Parents who constantly remind their sons that they really must express their feelings may unintentionally cause their sons to feel pressured and anxious. If boys have nothing they'd like to say but believe they are supposed to talk anyway, they are likely to feel they are inadequate and that there's something wrong with them. One boy said he wished he could be hypnotized because he felt he had nothing to say but assumed there must be something within him that was special and needed to come out. An atmosphere of openness and honesty encourages expression of feelings for all children. Prohibitions of male tears and sadness or constant nagging about expressing emotions serve equally to close off your sons' (and daughters') feelings.

Providing male models for nonstereotypical professions should be a deliberate goal whether or not there are male role models in the family. Elementary age children rarely know male teachers except from physical education classes. They need to realize that men are teachers, artists, poets, authors, and composers of serious music (not only the rock variety). If they see their fathers cook, change diapers, and do child care, they can value the nurturant and creative sides of their own personalities. If only the macho

154

image of males is projected, then gangs and sports become the only outlets for male identification.

Single mothers can be important role models for their sons, but it is very important developmentally for boys also to have male role models. This can feel frustrating for women who don't have fathers, brothers, or male friends to be supportive to their parenting. Social agencies often assist in encouraging adult males to volunteer leadership and companionship for boys. Support groups for parents of gifted children can also provide an excellent source of effective male role models. Fathers can share their interests and skills with groups of gifted children to encourage challenge experiences for all gifted children while also being role models for boys who may not have their own fathers.

Most critical of all, boys need to hear and see men showing respect for women as equal partners. This guides them toward respecting and valuing their mothers, their wives, their female colleagues, and other women.

38

~~~~~~

PEER PRESSURE

For gifted achieving students, the middle school years may be a most difficult time. From about fifth grade on there is considerable peer pressure on preadolescents and teenagers to "fit in" with the popular crowd and be accepted by peers. This pressure often seems more extreme for females than it does for males, although most children experience some conflict. On the one hand, they'd like to excel in their activities; on the other hand, they are not certain if their excellence is acceptable to their particular group of friends. They often find themselves torn between developing their talents and hiding these same abilities and efforts for the sake of acceptance.

Special vocabulary that labels students who appear too studious has varied through generations. "Brain," "nerd," "schoolboy (or girl)," "bookie," and "geek" are some of the uncomplimentary terms used to describe serious students who don't fit in with the popular crowd. African-American youth who study may be teased as "acting white," and Native Americans are often called "Apples"—red on the outside and white on the inside. These terms can cause a good student to develop a high-risk behavior. Preadolescents may be teased cruelly and even physically abused by groups of other students who do not accept the personality and interest differences of those who are serious about learning and who seem to care only a little about social life. Serious students often feel isolated and unacceptably different. Here is an example:

Scott explained the "customs" that fifth graders were expected to adhere to, including special ways to wear socks, ways to sit and not to sit, appropriate food to eat at lunch, and appropriate standards of casualness. He said he didn't want to "do" the customs, but he was afraid the kids would beat him up if he didn't, as they had his friend. He was also unwilling to let the psychologist talk to the teacher about the pressured activity.

Girls who are extremely attractive and boys who are excellent athletes sometimes have enough status to manage both to excel and fit in. However, because teenagers rarely have a great deal of social confidence, hiding one's talents is a fairly frequent behavior. Some children copy, cheat, and are defiant to fit in with friends who are doing the same. Your children's problems can become much more serious as they lose skills and academic confidence.

Typically, parents and teachers are very concerned about their children's social adjustment; perhaps they're overconcerned. They often become anxious if their children don't have friends or aren't popular and even brag about their social successes. Parents and teachers discuss social issues frequently, either with their children or students or with other adults within their children's hearing, sending messages that social acceptance is a high priority. Here are some examples:

- If children don't want to go out for recess because they'd rather stay in and read a book or work on a science project, teachers usually insist that they go out with the others. Children should be able to make the choice to stay in and continue the intrinsic interest.
- Most teachers or administrators, when consulted about possible grade skipping for highly gifted children, first ask about the social adjustment involved in such a decision. Parents

and teachers may actually use concerns about social adjustment as a basis for not providing academic challenge. Social adjustment seems to be their number one priority.

- If children play alone or have only a few friends, both teachers and parents tend to encourage them to join others or invite friends to their homes almost as if they fear that children who are not popular will not be successful.
- Parents and teachers continuously redirect independent activities to social activities and praise the more social children in the family or in the class.
- Parents often say repeatedly that they don't want to move to a new city because their children will lose their friends or they don't want to move to the country because they might be away from friends. They tend to want to be sure there are friends available at all times for their children, as if their children might suffer if they live away from other children.

Peer pressure against learning is a very serious problem in our country. You don't want your children to be without friends, but these are crucial years for teaching them a value system that surely includes honesty and achievement. Don't "wimp out" because you or they are afraid of their losing friends. Let them know early and often that everyone has to go it alone at times in life. Tell them that it is more important to stand tall and know that they are living by a standard of excellence and honesty than to conform to a peer standard that in the long haul will cause problems. Let your children know that it's all right to walk the school halls alone because this will equip them to be strong.

You can't prevent your children from feeling pressure in most middle schools unless you encourage them to conform to an antilearning standard. This is an opportunity to give your children a powerful message about independence and moral strength. Although it is difficult for you to watch your children struggle to maintain values of integrity, honesty, individuality, and love of learning, these are values that will begin to pay off for them in only a few more years. Here are some helpful messages that teachers and counselors have shared with me:

- Explain that the nerds of today will own the Lamborghinis of tomorrow.
- Explain that after grade 12, no one cares who was popular in middle or high school.
- Try this "what do you call" joke:

    Counselor: What do you call a student who studies hard, talks to the teacher after the class, does extra work, does more than expected, and wants to do his or her schoolwork?

    Student: Nerd, brain, geek.

    Counselor: What do you call adults who work hard at their jobs, do more than expected, want to meet high standards, and are interested in their work?

    Student: Gee, I don't know.

    Counselor: You call them "boss."

When parents prioritize social adjustment, they are also unintentionally giving a message to conform socially. Their children may be the first to get involved in drinking at parties because they want to fit in and are worried about popularity.

Let your children know that it will pay off to be strong despite peer pressure. Help them search out other students who share similar interests so that they don't feel so alone. Encourage your children's involvement in positive school activities in which they can share fun learning with other students—such activities as band, drama, forensics, computer club, school newspaper, and Future Problem Solving. Your children's positive involvement will help them through the peer-pressured days of middle and high school. Usually, by eleventh grade, the negative peer pressure diminishes, and the academic goals you've worked so hard to encourage in your children are now also respected by their peers. By the time they get to college, the nerds and the popular students intermingle. Gifted achieving students in college are not destined to wear "I was a geek in high school" on their foreheads. Nerdiness will be forgotten, and your children's academic achievement will open doors to their futures.

39

GRADE PRESSURES
AND TENSION

All children receive some form of evaluation and feedback from their teachers about their school progress. The communication that describes children's school progress is usually shared directly with parents (except at the college level) in the form of report cards. Although grades are not the only source of pressure for intellectually gifted children, they can certainly cause tension for these children despite their excellent capabilities. Small amounts of tension are not harmful and are indicators only of reasonable motivation. It is when tensions mount to the extent of causing such symptoms as nail biting, headaches, stomachaches, or generalized anxiety that clear indicators of problems present themselves. Often the children who exhibit these tensions in fact have good grades, although this is not always the case. Furthermore, when parents observe their children's tension symptoms, they may even feel guilty because they believe that they are causing their children's feelings of pressure.

Sometimes parents can pressure their children by their overpraise, rewards, and excitement about their children's grades. Of course, it is appropriate to show enthusiasm for high grades, or children believe that their grades don't matter to their parents. However, continuous all-A report cards can cause children to feel that these are the only acceptable report cards unless parents temper their excitement with explanations to their children. After all, an all-A report card leaves no room for improvement but much reason to fear lower grades in the future. It is unlikely to cause pressure in the elementary grades, but as the curriculum becomes more complex and competition increases, gifted children may actually fear receiving their first B.

Parents' discussion with their children about report card grades, the content of their children's learning, and the progress in their efforts permits parents to communicate their important concerns about learning and effort. These discussions can also relay the message to children that challenge involves learning from mistakes and that the curriculum and assignments will become increasingly difficult as students advance in grades. Parents need to guard against overreaction to either excellent or poor grades. Rewards and punishments for grades do little to motivate children. Joint problem-solving strategies are much more effective.

When parents respond to their children's tensions in regard to grades with "grades don't count as long as you're learning," they may be initiating a difficult set of problems. Grades count for college scholarships, honors, and for opening up many other educational opportunities for your children. It is too easy for your children to take literally any lack of concern for their grades. Gifted children too often assume that they should learn only that which interests them. Although parents should certainly encourage the pursuit of their children's interests, they also need to be required to meet general academic expectations. Parents often become confused in their messages because they want to avoid pressuring their children.

Grades count; however, they certainly aren't all-important. "Effort," "initiative," "attitude," and "interests" are terms that can guide your children along a balanced and motivated pathway.

Encourage your children to talk through their grade concerns with you rather than build internal tensions. If they don't initiate the conversations, you should, or they may make assumptions about your expectations that are unfair to themselves and to you.

A balance of physical exercise and recreational activities can help your children to cope with physical tensions. If children are showing extreme signs of pressure, counselors may help them to understand their feelings. They may also teach them relaxation exercises or use hypnotherapy or biofeedback to teach them to cope with pressures.

Sometimes children exhibit symptoms of tension when they are not even working to their abilities in school. Assignments that have not been turned in, unwritten term papers, and procrastination may cause children to feel more tension than when they are actually working at their assignments. Even intellectually gifted children can feel overwhelmed by thoughts of what they believe they are supposed to accomplish but feel unable to. They easily set their goals impossibly high. Reassuring them that they will be able to complete an A^+ paper may only backfire and cause them to feel even more pressure. If your children feel overwhelmed by long-term assignments, it's best initially to help them break up their projects into shorter daily assignments so that they can monitor their steps of progress and even share them with you.

Students who accomplish much in our society experience tension and pressure at many junctions. Parents can't protect them from these pressures, but they can help to place them in perspective. Furthermore, it's quite important that parents not add unnecessary unrealistic pressures to those that their gifted children may already feel. Parents in general try hard not to pressure their children, but sometimes, in the

163

excitement of their gifted children's accomplishments, it is difficult not to set continuously higher expectations. Parents who conscientiously try to keep good communication with their children are more likely to be sensitive to when they need to modify expectations to assist children in feeling motivated without feeling unreasonable pressure.

40

UNDERACHIEVEMENT

Intellectually gifted children who do not work to their abilities in school are underachieving. They frustrate their parents and teachers because they are obviously capable of satisfactory achievement. Most teachers, and even parents, concur that underachievement appears to be reaching epidemic proportions.

Unfinished work, disorganization, excuses about forgotten assignments and homework, a disinterest in most academic subjects, and a description of school as boring or useless are the initial indicators of underachievement syndrome. Other characteristics that may also be typical of these children are poor study skills, uneven abilities, high creativity, lack of perseverance, procrastination, perfectionism, and escapes to books, television, video games, or social life.

Underlying the surface characteristics that these children exhibit are two main characteristics. First, underachievers have not regularly experienced the relationship between their own personal efforts and educational outcomes (internal locus of control). Second, they are so highly competitive that they don't dare take the risk of making an effort for fear they will fail to meet their own too high expectations.

Underachieving children often have expansive but unrealistic dreams of being, for example, famous, millionaires, rock stars, or professional football players, but have not learned the discipline or goal setting required to arrive at these dreams. They make protective excuses rather than take the risk of carrying out the activities that are necessary to fulfill more realistic goals.

Underachievers have a great many bad habits that they have developed to protect their fragile self-concepts. They unconsciously manipulate the adults in their lives, both parents and teachers, in ways that keep them feeling safe in the short run but plunge them deeper and deeper into underachievement. During the time when they should be benefiting from the learning experiences of school, they direct their energies toward avoiding learning. They manage to get parents and teachers to provide more help than they actually need (dependent underachievers) or they try to dominate adults by arguing, debating, and pushing limits (dominant underachievers). Sometimes underachievers combine dependent and dominant behaviors.

Adults (parents and teachers) who respond intuitively to underachievers often find themselves frustrated because these intuitive responses may only reinforce already harmful patterns. Counterintuitive responses are actually more helpful. For example, dependent underachievers, by both words and body language, request continuous help and exhibit symptoms of pressure despite adults' attempts to relieve pressures. As adults ease their burdens and do too much for them, their school achievement and self-confidence diminish further. In contrast, dominant underachievers tempt adults into conflict. As teachers and parents reason with them, they push limits until they perceive themselves to be winners. Intuitively, adults believe that they must convince these children of their position. The result is anger for both adults and children. Adults find themselves frustrated and either lose control or give in to children in exasperation. Children continue the "pushy," dominating arguing because they believe that there is a reasonable chance of emerging dominant. If adults become irrational and overreact with threats or punishments, children use this overreaction as a rationale for avoiding the responsibility requested by the adults. Furthermore, in their anger, they bring their problems to other unassuming adults, who then may either side with them or attempt to mediate the problem, giving them more power than the initial adult (parent and teacher) who was attempting to guide them.

Dominant underachievers are very powerful but often feel powerless. By adolescence these underachievers tend to have extreme mood swings related to their manipulative successes or failures. Figure 40.1 is a diagram of these types of underachievers. The children in the diagram represent only the characteristics of underachievement: these are not labels for children. Students in the lower quadrants have more severe problems than those in the upper quadrants.

Both home and school environments contribute to underachievement. Underachievement emerges when children feel they can't meet their own expectations or those of their parents and teachers. At home, contradictory messages by parents (see Key 3, "ogre and dummy games") ritualize a pattern of searching for the easy way out. In the classroom, insufficient challenge provides gifted children with the assumption that "smart is easy," and at a higher or more competitive level of curriculum that is no longer easy, they feel threatened by the new challenge.

Although the problems that lead to underachievement are complex, the behaviors are learned defense mechanisms; therefore, they can be unlearned. The reversal of underachievement is neither easy nor automatic but is certainly possible. Changes in family and school environments can help underachievers build confidence and become motivated to accomplishment. The flip side of the underachievement coin may indeed be "superachievement."

Figure 40.1
THE INNER CIRCLE OF ACHIEVERS*

Source: Rimm, S. *Underachievement Syndrome: Causes and Cures.* Watertown, WI: Apple Publishing Company, 1986. Reprinted with permission.

QUESTIONS AND ANSWERS

We have a four-year-old daughter who is very tall for her age and who wishes she could go to school every day. She is currently enrolled in a preschool, but her mid-September birthday would normally keep her from kindergarten until she's almost six. She loves school and is anxious to go.

Recent research shows that holding children back from kindergarten entrance doesn't help and may actually hinder their achievement.

Because your daughter's birthday doesn't meet the deadline, she would actually be entering kindergarten early. An individual evaluation by the school or a private psychologist can guide you in determining if she is academically ready for kindergarten.

Early entrance is usually recommended only if her IQ test scores are in the gifted range (above 130). If her test scores are within the average range, it is better to have her wait another year and to attend a good preschool program this year.

Our son, age nine and a half, has been identified as very intellectually gifted. He is concerned about his lack of friends. Sometimes my heart breaks for him when he talks about how some of the boys at school are mean to him. He is small for his age, shy, and not athletic at all. Our son seems old beyond his years. What should we do? I can feel his sadness.

It is difficult for parents to watch their children suffer, yet your boy is learning some hard lessons that he's likely to remember his entire life. It's fortunate that he's not good at everything. Children who are, are less likely to develop empathy for those who are less capable.

First, I suggest you reframe his loneliness as experience for independence. Explain that learning to be independent can be very difficult, but practicing independence at age nine is good preparation for his teenage years.

Second, insist that he get involved in some physical fitness activities. His poor coordination should not be used as an excuse to avoid physical activity. If he exercises regularly, his coordination is likely to improve.

Third, encourage your son's participation with groups of children who share his interests. Children gain confidence when they have something they love to talk about.

As your son grows older, he'll find more friends with common interests, and he'll feel appreciative that you didn't pity him just because other children didn't accept him. For some very gifted children, differences are so extreme that finding peers is almost impossible. Beyond high school, social opportunities improve considerably.

This entire past school year has been a nightmare. My daughter is eleven years old and in sixth grade. Her last quarter grades were four Fs and one C. She is *not* a dumb kid. She doesn't do the work. Tests show she is in the 90th percentile. Her only interest is music. I had to take away her piano and guitar lessons for failing classes. My daughter told me that she is going to be a musician and doesn't need to learn what is taught in school.

A sixth grader who scores at the 90th percentile on achievement tests can have a bright future ahead, although a failing average surely indicates that she is in trouble.

Her message about wanting to become a musician and therefore sees no reason to learn what is taught in school is classic for underachievers but, nevertheless, provides a clue for motivating her.

It's a good idea to permit her to continue taking music lessons, *regardless* of her grades. Music will help her to retain some self-confidence and to understand the important relationship between personal effort and successful outcome. Furthermore, if she admires her music teacher, you may be able to ask the music teacher to confirm your message about the importance of school.

Try to convince your daughter to make a written commitment to devote a specific amount of time each day to study. Ask her to help design a study place in her room. If she would like to have some reward to help motivate her, attach the reward to regular effort and the completion of all homework each week. Don't reward grades. She may not have the confidence to maintain them and may give up when she receives her first poor grade.

A further precaution is that you can't expect your daughter to make a magical recovery despite her high test scores. Be patient, but hold her to her written agreement. Encourage her, and remind her of your trust in her.

I have a five-year-old son who has an IQ of 139. He is difficult to discipline, difficult for male children of the same age to get along with, and overly sensitive (angers easily). Can any of his socioemotional difficulties be attributed to his giftedness?

Many gifted children adjust well despite their giftedness, and some children with average abilities also have behavior problems. Although your son's giftedness is unlikely to be the only cause of his problems, it may be a contributing factor. For example, sometimes gifted children are overly sensitive because they have a heightened awareness to what others, including adults, may be saying. Gifted children who receive a great deal of recognition for their high intelligence may become highly competitive, which can interfere with social relations. Although it isn't possible to attribute your son's socioemotional problems directly to his giftedness, you are correct in assuming that there may be some critical connections.

I have some concerns about cooperative learning. When I was tucking our fourth grader into bed, she said, "I don't want to go to school tomorrow." She has been told that she is responsible for other children's grades because they're "study buddies."

There are claims that cooperative learning develops a better relationship between students of different levels. I've seen just the opposite. How do you feel about cooperative education for gifted children?

The term "cooperative" has such a positive connotation that hardly anyone disagrees with the concept that children should learn to cooperate. However, gifted children often complain about cooperative learning.

Some children feel frustrated when they believe they are taking most of the responsibility for work for which an entire group receives the good grade. Other children complain that they are required always to teach others and have little opportunity for learning. One student complained that he would get an F because the group would not include him in their project; another felt frustrated because he believed the group project was of inferior quality, and the teacher refused to accept his individual project.

Children should surely be involved in some cooperative learning experiences. The difficulty seems to arise when they become the main vehicle for children's learning. There is a great risk that children's individual needs will not be met and that students will feel pressured to conform to the group.

Cooperative learning experiences can provide valuable opportunities in every classroom, but when such group learning predominates in a classroom environment, this can eradicate creativity, individuality, and independence.

Our fourteen-year-old son has been accelerated into a class in which the students are older than he. He's become emotionally involved with a girl who is sixteen, and he seems to suffer because he doesn't have the social skills to pull off this relationship. Did we make a mistake by encouraging his acceleration?

You have no reason for regret. Your son's inability to attract a sixteen-year-old girl is unlikely to be related to his acceleration. Actually, all adolescents struggle with relationships that just don't work out. Occasional heartache and rejection are part of the dating game and are a healthy and normal part of growing up as long as they're balanced with other reasonable relationships.

You may wish to comfort your son in his frustration about his social problem, but please don't blame it on his acceleration, or he will. By the time he gets to college, your son's age will seem much less important than his intellectual competence, interests, personality, and character.

The school districts in my area are moving toward dropping honors classes in the high schools. The rationale behind this movement includes the following: (1) provide the same educational opportunities for all, and (2) use brighter achieving students as role models for underachieving or slower students and students with behavior problems. What do you think of this trend?

Schools seem to follow predictable cycles for honors classes and academic achievement grouping. The present thrust in this cycle emphasizes teaching all children similar material in heterogeneous groups. The effect of not challenging more capable children will register fairly quickly on standardized achievement tests and in the frustration levels of gifted children and their parents. Complaints are being heard already. To treat all children the same is to deny the concept of individual differences.

I have a teenage son who, as a high school senior, has been identified as a gifted underachiever. He has had many problems with work completion. We have requested that teachers accept late assignments, even though he may not get the credit for the grade. They have refused, stating that it's just too much work for them.

Senior year is a late starting time for reversing underachievement, yet working with your son at the threshold to higher education may show results in college. First, explain to your son that your purpose is to help him prepare for college. Then, indicate to him that his assignments are intended to be learning experiences whether or not they are graded.

Arrange to meet with each of your son's teachers separately, and explain your concern about his preparation for college. Affirm your support for their teaching. For subjects in which there are missing assignments, ask if you can call them on Friday afternoon to keep your son accountable.

Next, explain your accountability plan to your son and your determination to help him positively with his long-standing study problem before he leaves for college. You can tell him that if all of his work is handed in on a timely basis, you will permit him to drive the family car on the weekend; if not, you won't. If there are unfinished assignments, require him to complete them before his weekend social life begins.

When he furiously reminds you that you are being too controlling and are treating him like a child, humbly agree, and explain that you'll be happy to back away as soon as he demonstrates consistent responsibility.

GLOSSARY

Academic acceleration moving through curriculum material more quickly by compacting lessons, skipping to a higher level in a subject or grade, entering school early, taking college-level courses in high school, or actually entering college before the typical age.

Academic enrichment expansion of the curriculum within a particular grade level by including more in-depth material than would normally be included at that grade level.

Advanced Placement (AP) Courses college-level courses that are available to high school students at many high schools. They are sponsored by the College Board.

Attention deficit disorder (ADD) difficulty with concentration.

Attention deficit-hyperactivity disorder (ADHD) difficulty with concentration, high energy, and impulsive behavior.

Ceiling scores the highest possible scores attainable in a particular test. It is often difficult to differentiate among highly gifted children because their achievements and aptitudes exceed typical approaches to testing. Tests are often simply not difficult enough to measure their academic achievements.

Developmental delay uneven development in which some kinds of maturation happen later than others. Developmental delay assumes that there will be catch-up later in that development.

Grade-equivalent score the score on a test that is average for children at that particular grade level; for example, 10.8

means that a child has scored on a particular test similarly to average children in the tenth grade, eighth month.

Heterogeneous grouping children of all ability or achievement levels working together in one group.

Home schooling education conducted at home by a family member in lieu of attendance at school.

Homogeneous grouping children learning together who are in a similar achievement or ability range.

IQ Tests Such tests were originally thought to measure actual intelligence. IQ stands for *intelligence quotient*, which was the relationship of mental age divided by chronological age. The quotient was multiplied by 100 to obtain the IQ score. Thus, a child who was ten years old and passed tests at the fourteen-year-old level was said to have an IQ score of 140 ($14/10 \times 100 = 140$). IQ tests are no longer considered actually to measure intelligence, but they predict school achievement fairly well. An IQ score above 130 is considered in the very superior or gifted range.

Multipotentiality many high abilities that are quite different from one another. Having such a variety of high talents can confuse young adults as they try to select careers.

Perfectionism the setting of impossibly high standards paired with feelings of inability ever to accomplish these standards. Perfectionism differs from excellence in that the latter represents a high quality that is possible and provides the person with satisfaction.

Plug lock a lock that can be purchased to control television or computer games. The plug is taken from the wall and placed into the lock to prevent children from watching television when unsupervised.

Reading disability difficulty with reading material that is appropriate to the child's intelligence level.

School phobia fear of attending school.

ADDITIONAL READING

Adderholdt-Elliott, Miriam. *Perfectionism*. Minneapolis, MN: Free Spirit, 1987.

Bloom, B. S., Editor. *Developing Talent in Young People*. New York: Ballantine Books, 1985.

Davis, Gary. *Creativity is Forever*, 3rd Ed. Dubuque, IA: Kendall/Hunt, 1992.

_____ and Rimm, Sylvia B. *Education of the Gifted and Talented*. Needham Heights, MA: Allyn & Bacon, 1993.

Hart, Avery, and Mantell, Paul. *Kids & Weekends*. Charlotte, VT: Williamson, 1992.

Jones, Claudia. *Parents are Teachers, Too*. Charlotte, VT: Williamson, 1988.

_____ . *More Parents are Teachers, Too*. Charlotte, VT: Williamson, 1990.

Kerr, Barbara A. *Smart Girls, Gifted Women*. Columbus, OH: Ohio Psychology Press, 1985.

Parnes, S. J. *The Magic of Your Mind*. Buffalo, NY: Creative Education Foundation, 1981.

Rimm, Sylvia. *Underachievement Syndrome: Causes and Cures*. Watertown, WI: Apple Publishing Co., 1986.

_____ . *Marching to the Beat of a Different Drummer*. Gifted Child Today, *10* (1), 1987.

_____ . *Why Do Bright Children Underachieve? The Pressures They Feel*. Gifted Child Today, *10* (6), 1987.

_____ . *Gifted Kids Have Feelings Too*. Watertown, WI: Apple Publishing Co., 1990.

_____ . *How to Parent So Children Will Learn*. Watertown, WI: Apple Publishing Co., 1990.

_____ . *A Bicycle Ride: Why We Need Grouping*. How to Stop Underachievement Newsletter, *1* (3), Educational Assessment Service, Inc., 1991.

_____ . *Teaching Competition to Prevent and Cure Underachievement*. How to Stop Underachievement Newsletter, *2* (2), Educational Assessment Service, Inc., 1991.

_____ . *Sylvia Rimm on Raising Kids*. Watertown, WI: Apple Publishing Co., 1992.

_____ and Lovance, Katherine J. *The Use of Subject and Grade Skipping for the Prevention and Reversal of Underachievement. Gifted Child Quarterly, 36* (2), 1992.

_____ and Lowe, Barbara. *Family Environments of Underachieving Gifted Students. Gifted Child Quarterly, 4* (2), 1988.

Smutny, Joan F., Veenker, Kathleen, and Veenker, Stephen. *Your Gifted Child.* New York: Ballantine Books, 1989.

Treffinger, D. J., Isaksen, S. G., and Fierstien, R. L. *Handbook of Creative Learning.* Williamsville, NY: Center for Creative Learning, 1982.

Webb, James T., Meckstroth, Elizabeth A., and Tolan, Stephanie S. *Guiding the Gifted Child.* Columbus, OH: Ohio Psychology Press, 1982.

Books and Materials to Encourage Gifted Girls

Aristoplay. *Great Women* (card games). Ann Arbor, MI.

Boter, Mary C. *Women Who Made History.* London, NY: Warne, 1963.

Boynick, David. *Women Who Led the Way: Eight Pioneers for Equal Rights.* New York: T. Y. Crowell, 1959.

Downie, Diane, Slesnik, Twila, and Slenmark, Jean Kerr. *Math for Girls and Other Problem Solvers.* Eureka Catalog, 1985, ©1981 The University of California.

Epstein, Vivian Sheldon. *The ABC's of What a Girl Can Be.* Denver, CO: VSE Publisher, 1980.

Epstein, Vivian Sheldon. *History of Women for Children.* Denver, CO: VSE Publisher, 1984.

Epstein, Vivian Sheldon. *History of Women Artists for Children.* Denver, CO: VSE Publisher, 1987.

Johnston, Johanna. *They Led the Way: Fourteen American Women.* New York: Scholastic, 1973.

Marsh, Carole. *Math for Girls: The Book with the Number to Get Girls to Love and Excel in Math.* Berkeley, CA: Gallopade Publishing Group, 1989.

Moore, E. K., Vassell, M. A., and Wilson, J. *Beyond the Stereotypes: A Guide to Resources for Black Girls and Young Girls.* Washington, DC: National Black Child Development Institute, 1987.

Ross, Pat. *Young and Female: Turning Points in the Lives of Eight American Women.* New York: Random House, 1972.

RESOURCES

General

Consultant for Gifted and Talented
State Department of Education
Your State Capitol (You will wish to check for more detailed address)

Council for Exceptional Children–The Association for the Gifted (CEC-TAG)
1920 Association Drive
Reston, VA 22091

Educational Assessment Service, Inc.
W6050 Apple Road
Watertown, WI 53098

ERIC Clearinghouse on Disabilities and Gifted Education (provides free information)
1920 Association Drive
Reston, VA 22091

Gifted Advocacy Information Network, Inc. (GAIN)
225 West Orchid Lane
Phoenix, AZ 85021

Gifted Child Society, Inc. (PING)
190 Rock Road
Glen Rock, NJ 07452-1736

National Association for Gifted Children (NAGC)
1155 15th Street NW
Suite 1002
Washington, DC 20005
(202) 785-4268

World Council for Gifted and Talented
Membership Services
Purdue University School of Education
1446 LAEB
Room 5167
West Lafayette, IN 47907-1446

College Board Offices

For information on Advanced Placement courses and the College Level Examinations Program, please contact the following:

Denver Office
Suite 23
2142 South High Street
Denver, CO 80210
(303) 777-4434

Middle States Regional Office
Suite 1418
1700 Market Street
Philadelphia, PA 19103
(215) 567-6555

Midwestern Regional Office
1 American Plaza
Evanston, IL 60201
(312) 866-1700

New England Regional Office
470 Totten Pond Road
Waltham, MA 02154
(617) 890-9150

New York Office
888 Seventh Avenue
New York, NY 10019
(212) 582-6210

Southern Regional Office
Suite 200
17 Executive Park Drive NE
Atlanta, GA 30329
(404) 636-9465

Southwestern Regional Office
Suite 922
211 East Seventh Street
Austin, TX 78701
(512) 472-0231

Western Regional Office
800 Welch Road
Palo Alto, CA 94304
(415) 321-5211

Tests and Identification Instruments

Achievement Identification Measure (AIM). Watertown, WI: Apple Publishing Co.

Achievement Identification Measure–Teacher Observation (AIM-TO). Watertown, WI: Apple Publishing Co.

American College Testing Program (ACT). Iowa City, IA: American College Testing.

Baldwin Identification Matrix. Monroe, NY: Trillium Press.

Frasier Talent Assessment Profile (F-TAP). Mary Frasier, University of Georgia.

Group Achievement Identification Measure (GAIM). Watertown, WI: Apple Publishing Co.

Group Inventory for Finding Creative Talent (GIFT). Watertown, WI: Apple Publishing Co.

Group Inventory for Finding Interests (GIFFI). Watertown, WI: Apple Publishing Co.

Henmon-Nelson Tests of Mental Ability. Chicago, IL: Riverside Publishing Co.

Kranz Talent Identification Instrument (KTID). Moorhead, MN: Moorhead State College.

Otis-Lennon Mental Ability Tests. San Antonio, TX: Psychological Corp.

Preschool and Kindergarten Interest Descriptor (PRIDE). Watertown, WI: Apple Publishing Co.

Purdue Academic Rating Scales (PARS). Monroe, NY: Trillium Press.

Purdue Vocational Rating Scales (PVRS). Monroe, NY: Trillium Press.

Ross Test of Higher Cognitive Processes. Los Angeles, CA: Western Psychological Services.

SAT I. New York, NY: College Board.

Scales for Rating Behavioral Characteristics of Superior Students. Joseph Renzulli, University of Connecticut, Storrs, CT.

Slosson Intelligence Test. Odessa, FL: Psychological Assessment Resources, Inc.

SOI (Structure of Intellect) Learning Abilities Tests. Los Angeles, CA: Western Psychological Services.

Stanford-Binet Intelligence Scale Form L-M. Chicago, IL: Riverside Publishing Co.

Torrance Test of Creative Thinking–Figural. Bensenville, IL: Scholastic Testing Service, Inc.

Torrance Test of Creative Thinking–Verbal. Bensenville, IL: Scholastic Testing Service, Inc.

Wechsler Intelligence Scale for Children Revised (WISC-R). San Antonio, TX: Psychological Corp.

Wechsler Intelligence Scale for Children-III (WISC-III). San Antonio, TX: Psychological Corp.

Wechsler Preschool and Primary Scale for Intelligence–Revised (WPPSI-R). San Antonio, TX: Psychological Corp.

IMPORTANT PRINCIPLES

Principles for encouraging learning

1. Enjoy learning experiences with your children.
2. Provide books, resources, and early library opportunities.
3. Answer your children's questions, and give them the opportunity to find answers.
4. Ask your children open-ended questions that may have divergent answers.
5. Encourage and enjoy your children's sense of humor, and help them to laugh at their own mistakes.
6. Provide in-depth home enrichment opportunities.
7. Recognize the fine line that separates *support* from *pressure*.
8. Encourage active rather than passive learning.
9. Encourage some time alone in a quiet environment on a daily basis.
10. Identify mentors for your children, and be one for other gifted children.
11. Try to arrange a challenging school environment with your children's teachers.
12. Become directly involved in community support of gifted programs.

Principles for encouraging appropriate family structure

1. Stay united with your children's other parent(s), if there is another parent, and be willing to make compromises.
2. Give messages of respect for your children's teachers.
3. Be positive about your own career.
4. Encourage children to compete as good sports, but not only in sports.
5. Be a positive role model of activity, perseverance, and hard work.
6. Don't rescue your children from reality.
7. Place school effort and learning first, before sports or social life.
8. Keep a separate adult status for you and your adult partner without giving children adult status too soon.

INDEX